DESIGNING THE WORLD'S BEST
SUPERMARKETS

DESIGNING THE WORLD'S BEST
SUPERMARKETS

Martin M. Pegler

Visual Reference Publications Inc., New York

Copyright © 2002 by Visual Reference Publications Inc.

All rights reserved. No part of this book may be reproduced in any form or by any electronic or mechanical means, including information storage and retrieval systems, without permission in writing from the publisher.

Visual Reference Publications Inc.
302 Fifth Avenue
New York, NY 10001

Distributors to the trade in the United States and Canada
Watson-Guptill
770 Broadway
New York, NY 10003

Distributors outside the United States and Canada
HarperCollins International
10 East 53rd Street
New York, NY 10022-5299

Library of Congress Cataloging in Publication Data:
World's Best Supermarkets

Printed in China
ISBN 1-58471-025-X

Book Design: Harish Patel Design Associates, New York

CONTENTS

Introduction by Martin M. Pegler   7

Architectonics   9

CIP International   25

Danube Company Ltd.   41

Design Fabrications, Inc.   57

Heights Venture Architects, LLP   73

King Design International   89

Lind Design   105

Marco Design Group   121

Nebe International   137

Watt IDG   153

Project Index   170

Introduction

Supermarkets are a 20th century phenomenon and as we open the 21st century these markets are more attuned to the changing times than many other retail outlets. They reflect who we are and what we do today—and they even mirror our changing goals and aspirations. The supermarket is no longer the overgrown corner grocery or just a place to buy provisions. In many cases they have become mini-malls: an all-in-one shopping experience.

Today, shopping is THEATER; there are lights for ambiance, lights for attention and lights for appraisal. There are lights to give signage a splash and a dash and lights to enhance the color of the crisp green vegetables or give life to the seafood, or make the hot or cold prepared foods and salads seem more delectable. Designers design the supermarkets assisted by colorists, graphic artists, and lighting specialists. These supermarkets are being designed by image-makers—Brand Specialists—so that the store will project the right image to the targeted market which now includes the traditional "homemaker," the working mother or father, the single dweller, the teenager who shops for the family, and seniors.

Shoppers want choices, an in-depth selection, and value. They may prefer a bargain but will pay for what they really want. Like the department stores which the supermarkets are beginning to resemble (with their "boutiques" or specialty shops-within-the-shop), the market also wants to keep the shopper in-store longer and buying more. For this there are cafés, coffee shops, restaurants and even food courts within the supermarkets. Some are equipped with bank branches —or ATM machines—for the shoppers' convenience. There are video rental shops, drug stores, florists, party planning centers, etc. Supermarkets now anchor a small mall or hold down a strip center. They have become destinations; a place to meet—to see—to be seen—to eat—learn about health—sample new taste sensations and rediscover old ones. No longer is the supermarket drudgery; it has become fun—an adventure—and as the following projects will show—an experience.

For this, our first edition of "DESIGNING THE WORLD'S BEST SUPERMARKETS" we are pleased to present the work of ten outstanding architecture/design firms. They specialize in creating marketplaces. These leaders in the field share with us what they have recently accomplished and how the client's needs and desires were satisfied. As you study the projects presented you will see that the designers have worked to create stores with a "look" or "attitude," with an appeal to a particular customer or ethnic shopper. In this collection you will find markets especially designed for the cool climes of the Canadian Northwest as well as the color and sun-filled lands of Mexico and Puerto Rico. Our selections show stores in Argentina, Sweden, Saudi Arabia, and the United States. We feature many different types and sizes of markets with a variety of appeals; from the sophisticated to some designed for fun and the adventurous of spirit.

Sometimes working within limited budgets or in a less-than-perfect-for-the-purpose building, these architects/designers have successfully created the desired ambiance and attitude for the stores they designed. You will see the solutions in the decor, the graphics and the signage. Each firm's segment reveals how the designers approached the problem and achieved the desired brand results. Turn the pages slowly and savor the solutions.

Martin M. Pegler

Architectonics International Inc.
Retail Strategy   Store Design   Decor Design & Manufacturing   National Roll Out

285 Eastern Parkway
Farmingdale
New York 11735
888.753.Plan
516.753.3270
516.753.3273 (Fax)
designer@aiplan.com
www.aiplan.com

Architectonics International, Inc.

Evan's Supermarket
Detroit Lakes, Minnesota

Left: The produce area is accented with the colorful panels and special cart fixtures.
Below: The frozen food aisle is illuminated by two long rows of suspended fluorescent fixtures.

A monumental entranceway accents the wide, 62,000 sq. ft. building that houses Evan's Supermarket in Detroit Lakes, MN. The facade is decorated with colorful awnings that contrast with the neutral beige building which is located in a downtown area. The same upscale, neutral beige color sets the tone for the interior but the concrete floor helps to reaffirm the more popular price and value image the client wanted. The exposed, open joist ceiling supports the numerous suspended metal halide lamps that provide the ambient illumination while track lighting, with incandescent spots, is used for accenting. To maintain the desired "popular price" look, the fixtures and refrigerated cases are primarily covered with white laminates trimmed with black. The color in the design comes from the many hung panels that carry graphic images plus signage that identifies the product categories below. These two-sided, 3x6 ft. panels are printed in bright colors enriched with black. A checkerboard pattern is used throughout to unify the hanging signage as well as the horizontal wall signs. The signage makes movement through the space easy and also adds a "sense of discovery." Along with the friendly and inviting café and sampling stations, a "fun and festive feeling" fills the spacious market and has made it a popular favorite with the shoppers.

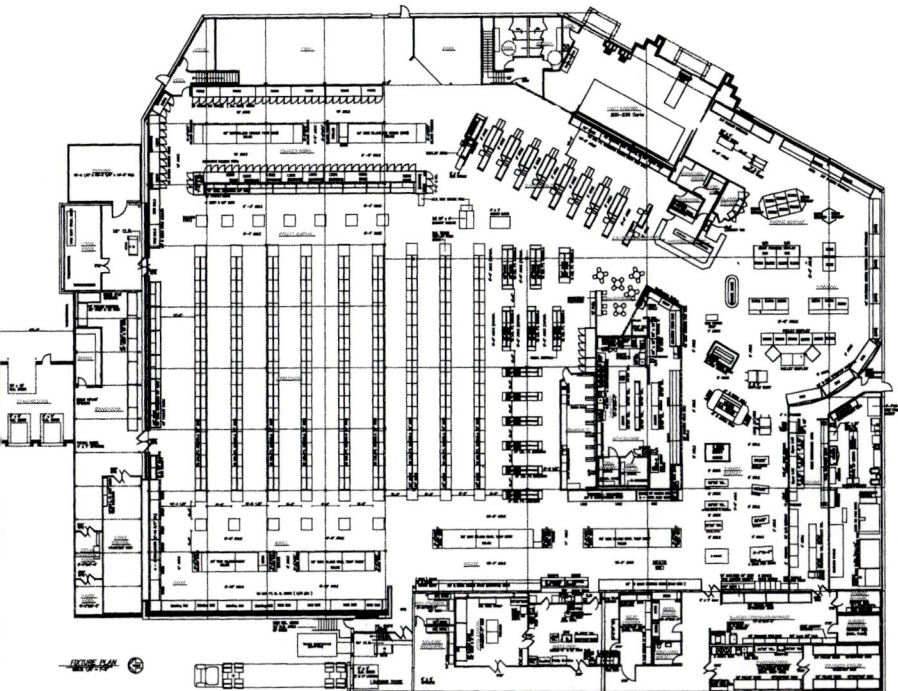

Above left: The customer service desk is located adjacent to the check-out counters.
Above right: The dairy area.
Center: The packaged meats department.
Below: The check-out counters.

11

Architectonics International, Inc. Nelson's Supermarket North Branch, Minnesota

Nelson's Supermarket in North Branch, MN is part of an independent, three-store operation. The client's request for the 59,500 sq. ft. modern, free-standing store with its scored stucco facade and expanses of glass and steel seemed simple enough—"Create a sense of discovery and visual excitement!" The "how-to-do-it" became the challenge for Architectonics, Inc. The store is filled with color, with light, with theatrical and dazzling eye-arresting architectural features, graphics and signage. Assorted shapes of floating ceilings hover over islands and some fan out from the perimeter walls to become attracting canopies that also carry the identifying signage. The giant white vinyl floor tiles are trimmed with black diamonds and that pattern is occasionally replaced by special designs such as the "cow spots" in the dairy department. The same decorative grid motif appears on the perimeter walls to unify the space while different colored ceramic tiles accentuate the individual service areas: blue in seafood, red in bakery, etc. The 18 ft.-high ceiling is covered with 2x2 tiles and high hat spots are recessed into the tiles. Ambient lighting fixtures are contained in the feature dropped elements or in the "skylight" over produce. Inverted, dome-shaped pendant lamps also serve as accents over special perimeter shops. "A combination of high tech materials such as perforated panels combined with the introduction of colorful and exciting colors not only complement the layout and reflect the exterior look but they are responsible for the 'WOW!' response from customers."

Above: *The grid scored facade that sets the decorative grid motif for the interior design.*
Center: *A fanning canopy of blue overhangs the seafood shop which is accented with blue tiles and decorative elements.*
Below: *The "cow-spot" floor set into the Dairy area separates it from the white + black grid shown elsewhere.*

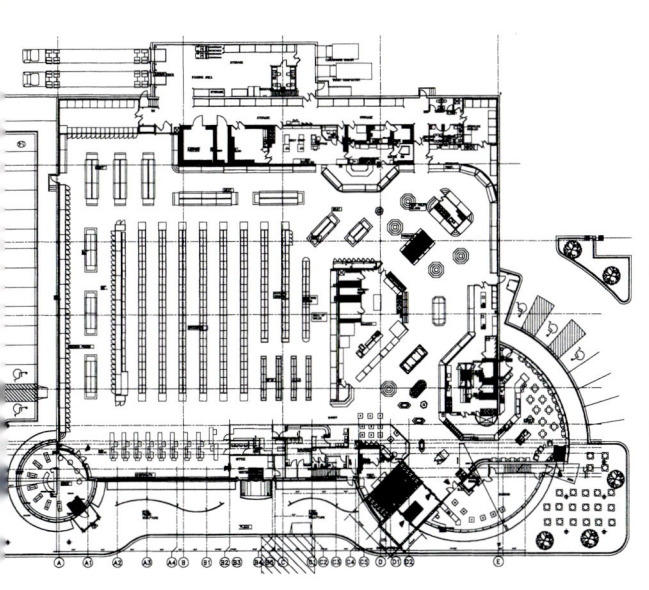

Above: The pizza island is one of the ready-to-go food areas in the food court.
Center: The entrance and nine checkout lanes.
Below: A palette of reds and oranges makes a big show for bakery. An illuminated drum carries the signage.

13

Architectonics International, Inc.

Rouse Epicurian Market
Thibodaux, Louisiana

To create the sort of warm, friendly and one-of-a-kind environment in the contemporary 62,000 sq. ft. space, the designers at Architectonics, Inc. relied on the flavor and color of New Orleans for their inspiration. The Rouse Epicurean Market is located in Thibodaux, LA and its spacious size combined with the soaring, open joist ceiling affect an airy and inviting ambiance filled with a rich, warm palette. Terra cotta walls, dark green, sleek black and handsome wood detailing take over under the suspended fluorescent fixtures which provide the general illumination.

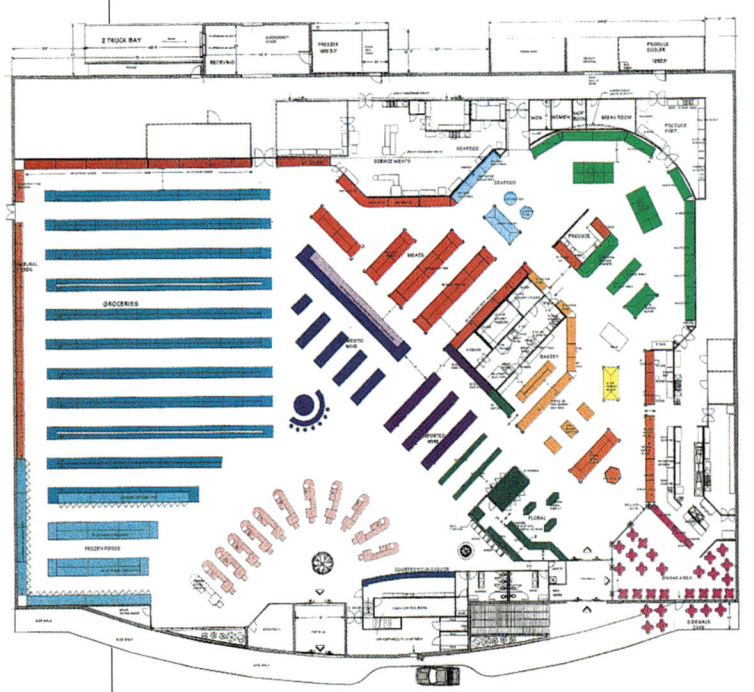

The signage and the decorative graphics that underscore and accentuate the New Orleans decorative theme, are accented by incandescent spots either on tracks or set into the dropped ceilings that help to delineate some of the special areas. Old fashioned, wrought iron street lamp-posts—a New Orleans signature—are furnished with directional arrows indicating the traffic routes to different parts of the market while the overhead banners, graphically enriched with photo blow-ups, provide further evidence of product location. Within departments, signs hung from fanciful iron brackets break down the departments into specialized product zones. Porcelain tile floors are used in the perishables department and assorted color-coordinated vinyls appear elsewhere. The market features an elegant wine shop, a floral area, a deli and "take-out" that provide Cajun specialties There is also a food court for the shoppers' pleasure and convenience. The success of this design led to another being built in Houma—30 miles north of this store.

Facing page, top: *The rich green color of the perimeter walls creates the fresh look for produce.*
Facing page, lower right: *New Orleans lamp-posts serve as directionals inside the store and add to the atmosphere.*
Above: *A sweeping aisle leads to 11 clearly-identified check-out stations.*
Center: *The elegant wine selection is housed on wooden fixtures under a wood grid filled with lights that add warmth.*
Below: *Pendant lamps highlight and define the service counters in the market.*

Architectonics International, Inc.

Park View Market
Bradford, Pennsylvania

Above: The new facade elevates the store's image yet still portrays "value and savings."
Left: The arched canopy defines the fresh produce wall display of product.
Facing page, Illustrated: The self-illuminated metal canopies over some of the specialty areas in the market.

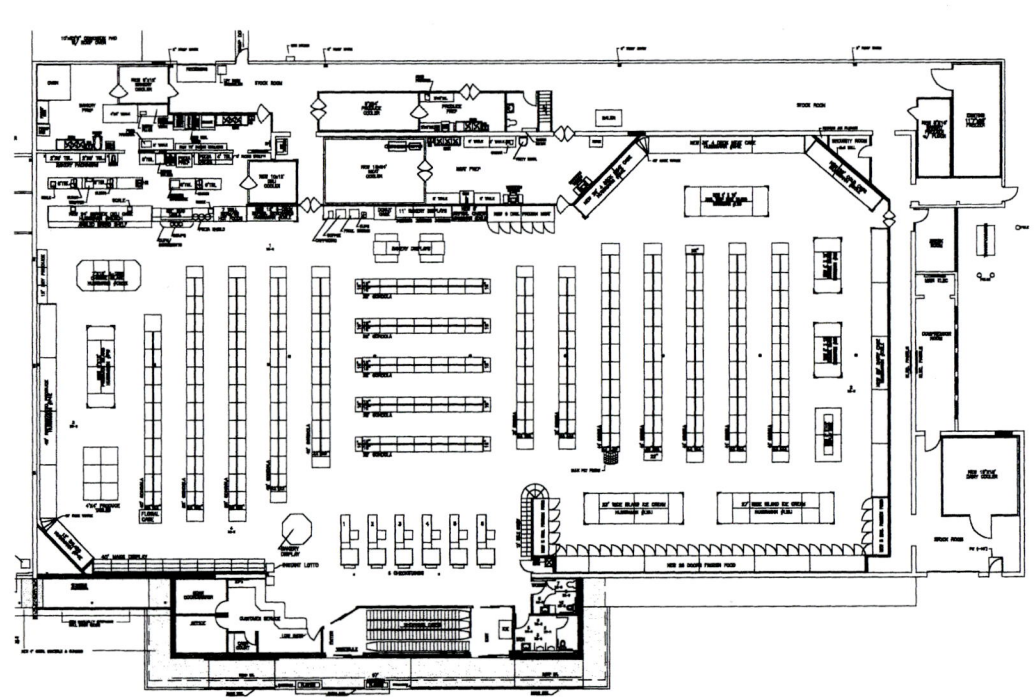

16

As described by the designer, Architectonics, Inc., "There is a touch of the classic" in this modern 27,750 sq. ft. Park View Supermarket in Bradford, PA. The client's request was for a store that the community would take pride in and one that would provide a feeling of "belonging and homeyness." In renovating the existing building, the low ceiling was a serious challenge since the client wanted "the store to feel open and bright and cheery." The 12 ft. space is now filled with warm, earth colors, faux painted walls and vinyl flooring laid in colorful patterns and trimmed with wood. Denish Doshi, president of Architectonics said, "We created a very strong presence on the outside and we wanted a similar feeling inside. We gave some of that outdoor feel to some of the departments inside." This was accomplished by the arched metal canopies that created partial "roofs" over the perimeter displays of product. Each canopy carries its own mini-spots to play up the wall-mounted signage and graphics. The designers also used art deco inspired decorative elements to add a sense of class and style to the interior as well as "open up" the space.

Architectonics International, Inc.

**Alfredo's Marketplace
Associated
Wyandanch, New York**

Above: Green letters set the theme for farmers market.

Below left: Giant number panels point out the checkout lanes

Below right: The deli is in gray with a yellow band accent that continues around and unifies the market.

Big, bold and punchy signage helps turn the 17,000 sq. ft. Alfredo's in Wyandanch, NY into a celebratory space where food and fun come together. The modern building for this Associated Market blends in with the community and thus has a sense of belonging. One of the major problems was the height of the space. In order to create a more comfortable and customer-friendly ambiance, the designers visually lowered the height by cutting it with wide and colorful bands of graphic signage that also delineate areas in the market. Though beige and pale gray cover most of the perimeter walls, it is the strong, vibrant colors of the giant letters that set the look for Alfredo's, and the largely ethnic community responds positively to the happy blues, greens, yellows and orange accents. The layout is simple. It is direct and makes the shopping experience a comfortable one. Wider aisles add to the comfort level as do the color coordinated vinyl floors except in the perishables department where porcelain is laid. Suspended metal halide lamps and track lights provide the major and accent illumination.

Architectonics International, Inc.

Seattle Coffee
Penn Station
New York, New York

Right and Above: The bright, sunny ambiance of the café in its underground location.

A stand-out in the rapidly expanding retail scene of Penn Station in midtown New York City is the Seattle Coffee Café/Take-Out which is located in a 1200 sq. ft. space. To create a warm and inviting area the designers painted, finished and furnished the café with a yellow-to-gold palette: from the huge signage drum suspended down in front of the semicircular counters and cases to the ceramic tiled rear wall and the circle-within-a-circle vinyl floor which is inlaid with the Seattle Coffee logo in green. Even the concrete slab ceiling is painted a sunny yellow. The Formica-faced counters are topped with granite and teardrop shaped lamps hang from the curved soffit that carries the product names. The overall effect has proven successful as "a gourmet takeout environment for a fast moving transit crowd."

Architectonics International, Inc.

Racemart
Raceway Petroleum
Highland Park, New Jersey

Part of the Raceway gas station is Racemart: a very attractive and convenient 1800 sq. ft. convenience store. Starting with the striking red, black and white metal facade, Architectonic, Inc. has "created a unique experience for customers who are accustomed to the ordinary." Inside, the semi-circular shape makes for a different kind of layout and the traffic is fluid and easy under the same kind of luminous ceiling as floats over the gas tanks outside. Light gray porcelain tiles cover the floor and the walls are pale beige. The red and black of the exterior are repeated inside along with wood cabinets and soffits. "The fun and colorful wall-mounted graphics and murals communicate directly to the customer-on-the-go" who is stopping off for refreshments. There is a self-service coffee corner, a "fixings" station and a Krispy Kreme donuts and muffins case as well as the curved walls of refrigerated cabinets filled with soft drinks, etc. This is definitely a "one-of-a-kind convenience store/gas station."

Above: The atmospheric, layered, wall-graphics/sign that locates the cold drinks zone.

Top: The semi-circular layout of the call cases that help create the fluid flow of traffic.

Right: The exterior of the convenience store and the luminous ceiling over the gas pumps.

20

Architectonics International, Inc.

Akbar's Café
New York, New York

Servicing commuters racing to and from trains and the multitude of hurried office workers in the surrounding skyscrapers, Akbar's Café provides smooth sailing for a fast moving crowd. The lime green serpentine soffit that undulates around the space and carries the names of the food stations in glowing neon signage ties the 5000 sq. ft. space into an easy-to-manage, self-service, shopping and dining experience. The exposed ceiling viewed beyond the dark ceiling grid is painted out. A white, free-form dropped ceiling around a free standing glossy red column anchors a focal self-serve food bar. The deep blue-green painted concrete floor is gridded to resemble ceramic tiles. Within the allotted space of this mini food court, diners can get anything from sushi to Mongolian grilled meats, gourmet deli, ice cream and juices as well as packaged food items to-go. Within the dark space, the signage and decorative elements in shiny red and bright green stand out. With the unique greenhouse seating and the open bar there is a feeling of a "happy hour" setting. "It is an oasis in the midst of a fast moving tide."

Above left: A view of the display cases and counters under the curving soffit.
Above right: The island food stand under the dropped white ceiling.
Right: Shiny red columns contrast with the green soffit. Note the dark grid that camouflages the real ceiling.

Architectonics International, Inc.

**Amelia's Market
Four Seasons, Indiana**

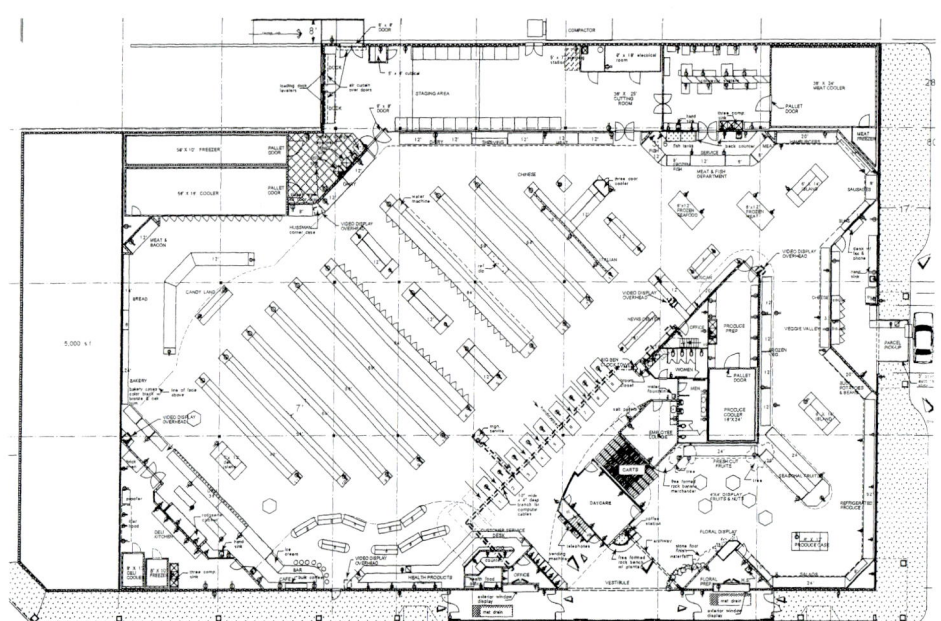

22

Amelia's Market is like no other market one is likely to see. It is like an epicurean voyage around the globe and Amelia serves as the guide and leads the food-seeking traveler to different ends of the world where ethnic delicacies are presented in clever and amusing vignette settings. The 45,000 sq. ft. market is located in Four Seasons, IN and Architectonics, Inc. created this eclectic interior where each area is defined by its colors, the ceiling drops, the unique vinyl floor treatments and the unusual decoratives and props. "It is a landmark store where a sense of discovery fills every corner." Giant trees—in full fruit—highlight the produce area. The fresh fruits are displayed in bushel baskets resting on octagonal steps of weathered wood as well as in the tiered wall cases. The area is illuminated by fluorescent fixtures set into the open grid ceiling and the focused incandescent spots. For this voyage—and for the shoppers' delight—the designers created a series of atmospheric environments that help set the scene for the various popular ethnic food specialties.

Facing page, left: Two full-size trees set the orchard/farm theme for produce.
Facing page, right: A giant frankfurter on a roll sits atop an island display of assorted picnic needs and sandwich fixings.
Below: The Asian Cuisine boutique is stocked with assorted Asian foods and condiments under a pagoda-topped fixture.

23

A Tower of Pisa, a gondola (the Venetian kind) and an Italian street scene become a shop-within-the-shop for Italian specialties. The red, white and green checkered floor of vinyl tile reinforces the Italian imagery. Metal halide lamps, suspended from the open joist ceiling, illuminate the pastas, sauces, oils, olives, and other imported delicacies. For the Asian cuisine, the designers created a full round, pagoda-style fixture and the Chinese tile roof continues as a frieze over the red and black lacquered shelving units. The red and black scheme is followed through on the floor where the bands appear to stretch the size of the shop. Oriental artifacts, vases, honeycombed papers, fans and such are decoratively used to enhance the setting.

If it is Fiesta time in Four Seasons, then Mexican and Latin American specialties are available in the colorful area filled with pinatas, Aztec temples and calendars, cacti plants and sombreros. Adding to the "adventure" and the pleasure of shopping Amelia's is the "drop-off" play area for the children and the food court where the international treats can be tried or tested. Amelia's Market has become a must-see, must-shop stop here in Indiana.

Above: The Italian cuisine department.
Right: The Latin American specialties zone.

CIP International, Inc.

9575 LeSaint Drive
Fairfield
Ohio 45014
513.874.9925
513.874.6246 (Fax)
cwhorning.cipstyle.com
www.cipstyle.com

CIP International, Inc.

Albertson's
Jackson Hole, Wyoming

With the Albertson's chain of supermarkets it all starts with creating a sense of community—a feeling of belonging—of being part of the neighborhood. That guiding premise is apparent in the design for the Jackson Hole market created by CIP International for the 57,985 sq. ft., uniquely shaped, freestanding store. For Thomas Huff, CIP International's CEO and Creative Director, it was an especially pleasurable challenge since he is so familiar with this community and thus he and his creative team set about to bring the "essence of the West" into the design of the total package. Since Jackson Hole has a strict code for architecture and signage, it was the designers' challenge to create a market that not only fit into the neighborhood but also exuded the "old West" feeling that the community revels in. In keeping with that, the market exterior is finished in natural woods, timber and earth tones.

Right: A huge rotating sign over the deli is topped with a two sided chef: one side has a male, the other, female. Behind is an "old west" streetscape of building facades.

Throughout the interior the designers maintained the old Western town look in the 20 ft. high space with an open ceiling. They used architectural motifs such as the house facades and variations on vintage signage—all executed in natural materials and colors—to accomplish the look. There are replicas of the famous Barn at Mormon Row, the pharmacy on Main Street, the movie theater marquee and even simulated wood plank sidewalks. Adding to the imagery are the bucking bronco, saddles and horseshoes inlaid in the flooring, the clapboard siding on the perimeter walls and the roof overhangs and cornices that are part of what we think of as an old West town. Because of the unusual shape of the building, the designers created a unique layout of shopping aisles—turned in different directions—"to bring a subliminal preparation in the customer's mind that sets up their purchase in the approaching departments."

Above right: *The end-of-aisle signs continue the "town" theme.*
Right: *The snack department is given prominence by the full round, huge bowl of snacks trimmed with a red checkered cloth liner suspended over the product display.*

27

Left: That is Elvis peeking out of the window of the Main St. building.
Below: The Main St. Florist is located in a "building" within the building. The "downtown"-inspired building also houses the pharmacy.

One of the outstanding decorative elements in the market is the 170 ft. long, mural of the Grand Teton Mountains which adorns the curved soffit at the left rear of the store. In front of the "mountain" is a replica of the Mormon Row Moulton Barn which serves as the feature element in the dairy area. The Hoback Bake Shop visually stakes out and takes over in the bakery area. Inspired by the local pharmacy, the designers created the attractive pharmacy facade to frame that department. Elvis Presley gets to peek from behind the window curtains that overlook the cold beverages stand. Holding this "community" together is the palette of soft warm neutral colors that run the gamut from creamy beiges and tans to deep earthy browns accented with subtle grays, terra cotta-red, ocher gold and cool blue. Azrock slip resistant flooring tiles are used in areas where may collect moisture and simulated wood flooring creates the cliché sidewalk of the 1880's Main St. and it runs in front of the pharmacy with staggered joints in the bakery and meats & seafood areas. Antique white tiles are used in the common areas accented with toast and gray.

All refrigerated cases are finished in black. The laminated fixtures for the service areas are finished in warm wood tones. In other service areas solid laminates are used that complement the product display. To light the space, decorative gooseneck light fixtures appear on the perimeter. Specialty track lights also highlight the major department signage and photographs arranged at the front of the store. A canned metal halide fixture system is utilized in the general sales area and frozen foods is highlighted with a strip fluorescent system set above a celled ceiling device that softens the illumination. The Reading Center has a fieldstone fireplace and pine timber tables and chairs, a snack bar, and a warm and welcoming delicious feeling of "home."

Above: The Hoback Bake Shop facade projects out over the aisle and features a collage of bakery products.
Below left: The focal point of the pharmacy is this framed department sign.
Right: Grand Teuton Mountains mural as backdrop of the store.
Below right: The replica of the landmark Moulton Barn in the dairy department is backed by the mural of the Grand Teuton Mountains.

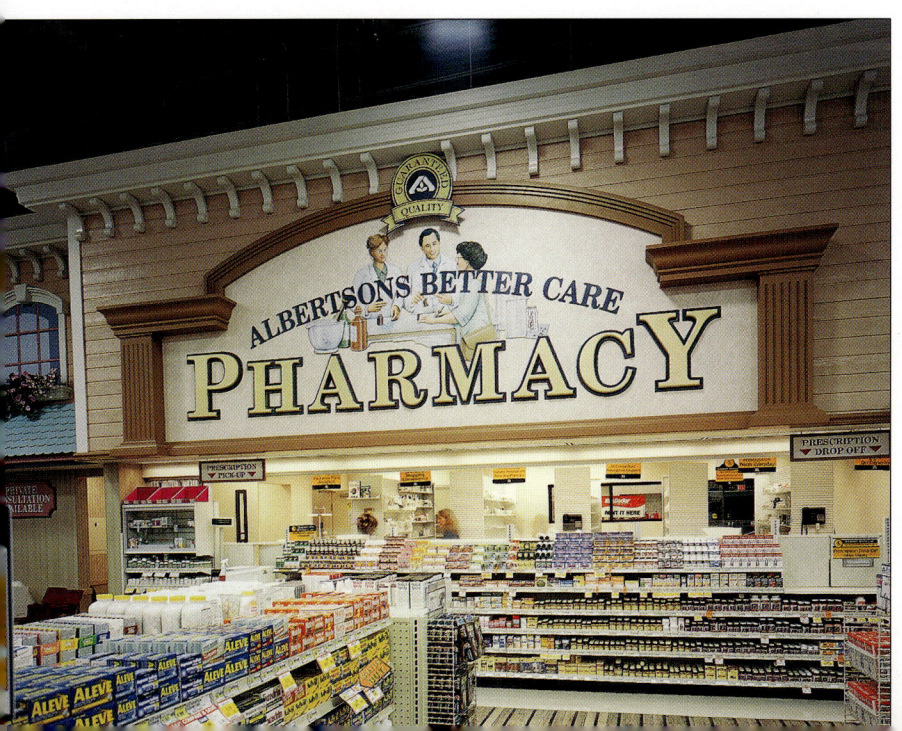

CIP International, Inc.

Trigs Food & Drug
Eagle River, Wisconsin

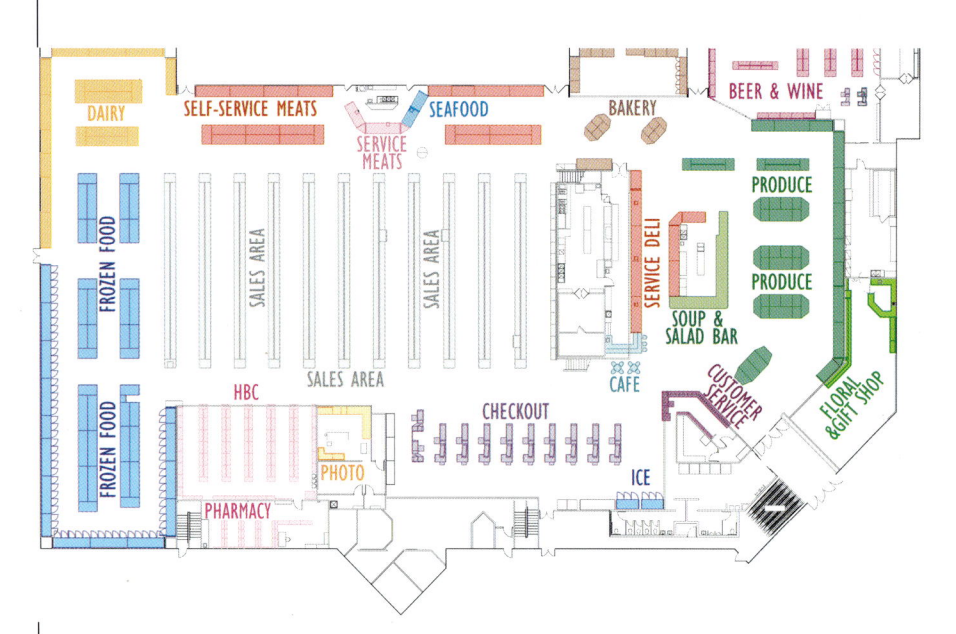

Left: An overview of the produce department, the giant mural on the rear wall, and the adjacent Roadside Stand.
Above: A detail of the produce wall mural, the simulated river rock wall covering, and the placards.

Trigs Food & Drug, a four-store chain in Northern Wisconsin, asked CIP International's CEO and creative director, Thomas Huff, to "design a store that brought the local 'northwoods' resort feel and architecture inside." The 73,000 sq. ft. store also had to have "a sense of excitement" for the many vacationing shoppers that visit and "a sense of pride" for the local residents who shop the store regularly. For Thomas Huff and his staff the challenge was fun. "One of the things that makes this store an interesting story is the fact that there are still places in this country for a themed store," says Thomas Huff.

From the hand hewn timbers to the rough sawn cedar to the realistic river rock and brick wall coverings to the oxidized metal awnings to the sandblasted wood signage—"this store is an experience in being in the 'north woods.'" There is even a 7x7 point bull elk trophy, taken by Thomas Huff himself, to greet shoppers in the meat & seafood department. The building is a new, free-standing 61,371 sq. ft structure and it is 22 ft. to the bottom of the joints in the open ceiling. Within the space CIP International created the warm and relaxed ambiance of a north woods lodge using mostly natural and native materials and earthy colors. Up front, near the entrance, is produce where the walls are clad with rough sawn cedar planking with weathered lettering painted over it to call shoppers to the Roadside Stand which is located under the oxidized metal awning. This creates an atmospheric setting for the fruits and vegetables stocked here. There is also a long mural of an orchard and farm over the perimeter wall gondolas. The mural is flanked by panels of simulated river rocks over which are set placards carrying the fresh fruits & vegetable message.

31

Left: *The meat & seafood service shop is a focal point and is accentuated by the bull elk mounted in the gable setting.*

Left below: *The meal-to-go island counter is highlighted by a double faced sign with the "A" frame motif. The specialty areas are delineated by simple signs at just above eye level.*

The individual service departments have been decoratively treated to further promote the north woods feeling. The meat & seafood shop has a framed, horizontal ship-lap, cedar siding fascia which serves as a background for the professionally hand illustrated wall murals above the burgundy colored metal awnings. Highlighting the area is the "A" frame gable—so typical of the north woods "lodge" architecture—with the aforementioned bull elk mount which calls shoppers to this department. The bakery has a faux finished brick wall covering with a mounted, inkjet simulated sandblasted wood sign. The aisle directories are all double faced with the "A" frame motif incorporated into the design and various names from the community are used to distinguish each aisle. The "A" frame concept also appears over the island counters and cases on the floor. Left: The meat & seafood service shop is a focal point and is accentuated by the bull elk mounted in the gable setting.

In contrast to the rough, earthy, natural materials and colors used on the fascias, soffits and awnings, the floors are covered with a neutral colored VCT tile. There are accent squares of burgundy and deep green used throughout the service areas and a medium brown, wood planking finish appears on the floor in front of meat & seafood, customer service and under the awnings of Tula's Deli. Painted areas of the store are white accented with hunter green, muted burgundy and midnight blue. The store is illuminated with an exposed fluorescent strip system suspended at 16 ft. for general illumination and metal halides are used over the center of the store. The wall department placards are spotlighted and halogen spots are used "to bring to life" the bull elk mount and the illustrations in meat & seafood. Other departmental signs are washed with strategically-placed fluorescent tube light. Recessed fluorescents are used in the bakery and pharmacy. Lee Guenther, president and CEO of T.A. Solberg Co. Inc., the store's operating company, said, "Obviously there's a lot of log structures up here and we wanted to make a statement with the log entryway." He got more than that and a much bigger statement was made: he got the entire "lodge" in a giant, well-designed package.

Right: The pharmacy: the brick wallcovering over the soffit adds depth to the dimensional gold lettering and the vacuum formed mortar and pestle.
Center: The brick covering also highlights the Northwood Bake Shop's inkjet "sandblasted" sign. All details are trimmed in rough sawn cedar.
Below: The deli shop is located beneath a fascia of rough-hewn wood and an oxidized metal awning. The hand-hewn railing above surrounds the sit down café where shoppers can watch the activity on the floor below.

CIP International, Inc.

City Market
Vail, Colorado

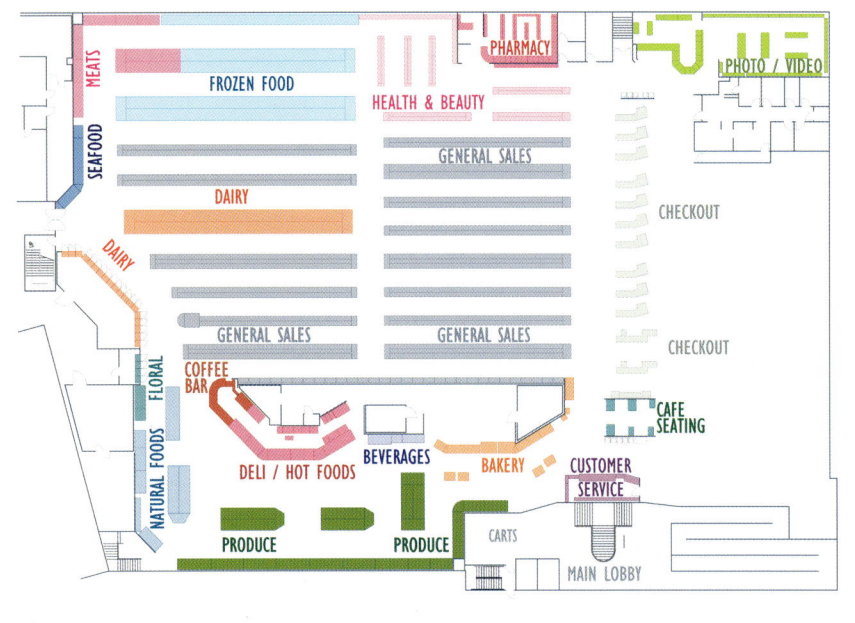

In keeping with its setting in Vail, CO and with the town's design review board who specified "different styles and textures" and "no long straight lines," CIP International came up with this European/Swiss chalet look for the 60,000 sq. ft. City Market. It is part of an integrated, middle income housing/retail shopping/parking development on city-owned land. The rich wood trim and off-white stucco of the exterior is accented with towers and variations in roof pitches. The interior has a ceiling 13.5 ft. above the finished floor and "the uniqueness of this design is that it needed to be responsive to the locals of this resort area while providing the expectations of the visiting tourists." Thomas Huff and his creative team chose a rich color palette to produce the desired upscale feeling and the "peaks, awnings, architectural details, graphics and fixtures brought it all to life." Rich burgundy, a gentle teal and soft mauve reappear as accents throughout. The white walls serve as a background for the fanciful chalet architecture used to delineate the service shops. A frieze of snow capped mountain peaks runs behind the chalets. The design of the Rockies, the peak framing of the chalets, awnings and the artwork of berries and flowers sets the look throughout. Dark wood accents, wood laminates and black refrigerated cases add to the upscale look and enhance the presentation.

Above and left: The espresso bar, features dimensional vacuum formed artwork contained within the pseudo-chalet framework. Above is the snow capped Rocky Mountains image that creates a frieze around the service areas. Gooseneck lamps extend out from below the cornice molding to light the shops and awnings. The floor tile accents and the awning colors help delineate the shops.

Right: Seafood & meat steps out from the back wall. The dark wood is accented by the teal/green awnings. The sign is dimensionalized with vacuum-formed fish, shellfish, poultry and steaks.

Below left: The fresh fish area turns the corner and the self-serve frozen seafood is available in the cases under the fresh sign.

Below right: Brightly colored flowers highlight the layered floral sign tied with a ribbon. The black espresso bar counter and the salad bar are complemented by the light flooring accented with soft teal and mauve.

CIP International, Inc.

Copps Food Center
Neenah, Wisconsin

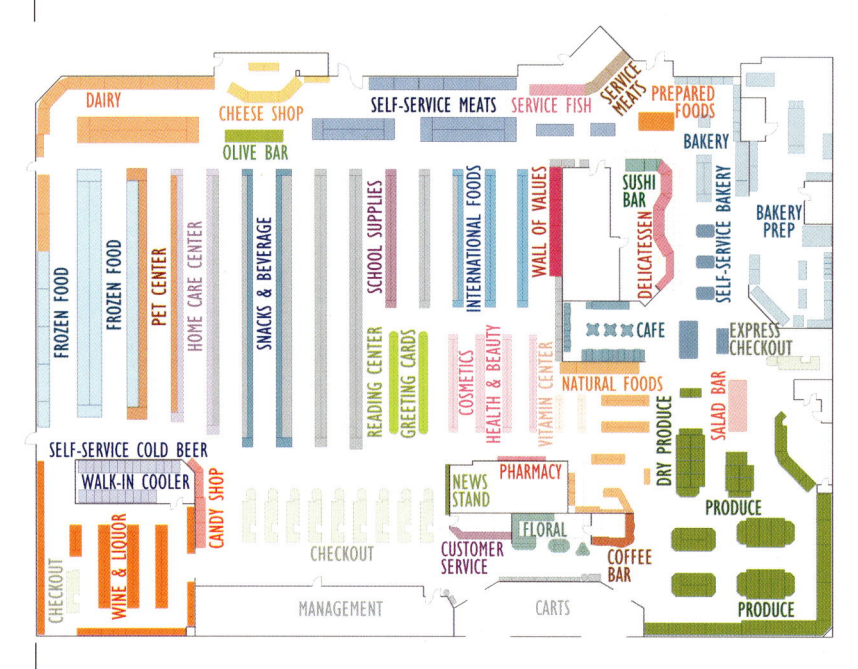

CIP International's Thomas Huff, working closely with Mike Copps and Ed Pliska of the Copps Company, came up with a concept and look for the Neenah, WI store that "redefines destination shopping." The layout, in the 58,485 sq. ft. space, was designed to take shoppers on a tour that goes from shop to shop to gather their needs. "This kind of shopping experience is meant to make a customer want to visit more often, and when they are here, feel good about buying more."

To set the ambiance and create the right mood, a tour of the perimeter of the store takes the shopper through a "village of shops." Each European-style shop is unique and special. "From the highly discernible copper awning in the deli, to the larger-than-life coffee cup over the coffee bar, to the exotic olive bar sporting dozens of varieties, to the specialty cheese shoppe where sampling is a way of life—the customer is enticed to see what is around the next corner."

Right: One of the two farm and orchard murals in the produce area. They are backed by the vertical wood plank siding on the wall.

The volume of the space feels enormous with the 22 ft. open bar joist ceiling across most of the store. The designers used the Gordon Architectural System to create a more "comfortable" 17 ft. drop around the perimeter of the market. Additional hard drops to 8 ft. were used to accentuate service departments such as seafood, meats and cheese. To overcome what might be a "cool atmosphere," "warmer areas" were created with specialty departments with rich, stained hardwood and simulated wood floors. The canopies, grills and trellises tend to lower the ceiling heights and affect more intimate spaces.

Twenty departments with 40 destinations were created to accentuate the destination market concept. By using the various ceiling drops, flooring patterns, architectural elements, wall treatments, color combinations, signage and lighting, the shopper moves easily and freely from shop to shop.

Above: The fresh fish market is located by the larger-than-life dockside mural that stresses the "fishing docks to your table" freshness.

Right: The olive bar: an upscale specialty area in the market located next to the specialty cheese shop. Add a splash of wine—also available—to set a convivial mood.

37

Customer convenience was not sacrificed in the design. An express entrance and checkout in the center area of produce/deli and bakery is "designed to give the customer the opportunity to visit the perishable departments for a speedy pick-up and be on their way quickly." There is another entrance and checkout located near the wine & liquor shop. The checkouts are made easily visible by a curved, full expanse metal grid system within a black and gold canopy. Destination departments were designed into a uniquely shaped arrangement to accentuate the highly profitable perishable departments. For shopper convenience, the flooring pattern follows the same outline as the Gordon architectural ceiling unit, which carries the track lighting and highlights the path. Linoleum and ceramic tiles were used in 17 colors and patterns, but it is the blue/gray flooring that follows the ceiling outline. White tile is used in the center of the general sales area while large black and white blocks dominate in the front of the store, through the perishable departments, down the side, and across dairy. Naturally stained wood-like tile covers most of the natural foods area. A diagonally laid pattern of alternating thin planking of medium and dark wood is in the wine cellar.

Above far left: Glistening copper awnings extend over the white refrigerated cases in deli. Lighting is from a track system of spots attached to the ceiling system.
Above: The wine cellar: Simulated red brick walls complement the dark wood fixtures topped with black laminates.
Below far left: The ends of the produce crates with their colorful labels are stacked against the timber wall to recall the "olden days." They complement the orchard mural in produce.
Below left: In frozen foods, "faded" wall murals and large lettering accent the unusual product identifiers.

39

Above left: Brick wallcoverings and raised louvered panels framed in natural maple, create the unique look for the bakery. Baked goods can be viewed through the openings.
Lower left: The giant coffee cup suspended over the coffee bar.
Lower right The metal mesh framed in a black grid spans over the check out counters. Above the mesh arch, the metal halide lamps provide ambient light.

A "sense of animation" is brought to many of the European-style shops through the larger-than-life decorative elements in the graphics program. There is a 9 ft. diameter coffee cup precariously tipped over the coffee cup bar with a drop of coffee suspended in time. The natural foods area is shaded by a huge pergola banded with steel rails to support the large dimensional lettering with replicas of natural food items perched on top. To set off the many decorative elements and signs, the upper portion of the walls throughout are covered with an inkjet wallcovering in a shaded diamond pattern in shades of mauve. The lower portions are tan stained wainscoting finish. All the refrigerated cases are finished in white with gray trim and the fixtures in the destination shops/departments are either in dark wood tones or neutral laminates. The store is illuminated with a canned metal halide system for ambient lighting and surface mounted and recessed directional spotlights are used to showcase the wall graphics and the individual departments. Chairman Mike Copps said, "This store is a labor of love. We have never worked so hard on concepts before but we really did our homework this time." The successful results are self-evident.

40

Danube Company Ltd.
Designed by: Mohammed Y. Al-Hasan

Heraa St. & Madinah Rd. Cross Section
P.O. Box 51280
Jeddah, 21543
Saudi Arabia
00966.2 658.0602
00966.2 654.1097 (Fax)
www.danubeco.com

Danube Company Ltd.
Designed by
Mohammed Y. Al-Hasan

**Danube Supermarket 5 Arbaeen
Jeddah, Saudi Arabia**

The elegant and contemporary facade on Prince Metab St. in Jeddah stands out from the surrounding retail stores, cafés and bistros. The designers made full and effective use of the hangar-like, 42,000 sq.ft. (3900 sq.m.) space, without columns, to create a spacious and inviting interior which has special appeal to the Asian and Indian expatriates who live nearby. The crisp, fresh, green and white palette that dominates in produce is accented with sunny yellow. Adding to the area's ambiance are the overscaled photo murals that reach from the produce counters to the ceiling. The on-the-floor produce, displayed in the specially designed circular stands, is illuminated from above by the custom green metal light fixtures. Produce is also set apart by the green vinyl tile floor and that same bright green is used to finish the long, metal gondolas that stretch along the perimeter wall. The salad bar is finished in a complementary green and is equipped with a sleekly-styled plastic sneeze guard. The rich blue back wall with a bor-

Above: The salad bar is finished in green and has a sleek sneeze guard.
Below: A long view of the produce area.
Left: A close-up look at the gondola. Note the angled mirror on the top shelf to highlight the merchandise.
Photography: Rasheed Babu and Adnan Juneid.

43

Top: The refrigerated cheese counter.
Above: The freshly-baked cakes and pastries are displayed in white cases trimmed in red.
Right: The meat department is dramatically set against a rich blue wall.

der design stenciled in gold makes a striking contrast to the red meats displayed in the contemporary-styled, self illuminated refrigerated cases. The gold color also appears on the back wall which is segmented by brass strips. Mirrors alternate with framed photographs in the formed panels. A metallic gold finish is used on the case supports and a foot rail, on the gray tiled floor, assure customer comfort while waiting for service. To enhance the display of meats, a series of incandescent flood lamps is lined up over the cases. Note the decorative Arabic artwork that is incorporated into the wall treatments.

A dramatic entranceway into the housewares area has been created by the deep blue, floor-to-ceiling piers and the angled proscenium of a lighter blue which is embellished with framed photographs of the merchandise set out beyond the opening. Special shelving units and gondolas were selected to furnish this area and the white tile floor and ceiling enhance the feeling of spaciousness. The brilliant blue wall that distinguished the meat department, previously shown, also sets the scene for this area as well as the spice boutique and packaged sweets zone.

The spices are displayed in easily accessible for self-service bins as is a scale for weighing the selections. A natural wood shelved "bookcase" unit with native carving trim holds the prepackaged spices, sweets and condiments as well as the glistening copper and brass roasters and grinders. According to the designers, "We were able to bring modern design combined with Arabic culture to the supermarket for our customer's satisfaction."

Right: The spice and sweets area is distinguished by the native wood shelved cabinet unit against the blue wall.
Below: The dramatic entrance into the housewares section of the Danube Supermarket.
Left, opposite page: Refrigerated cases stretching along entire wall.

47

Danube Company Ltd.
Designed by
Mohammed Y. Al-Hasan

**Danube Supermarket 3 - Tahalia
Jeddah, Saudi Arabia**

The upscale nature of the Thaliah St. location in Jeddah, is reflected in the refinement and elegance of materials and decor that are incorporated into the 23,700 sq.ft. (2200 sq.m.) supermarket. Marble and granite, fine woods and stainless steel accents, custom floor and lighting fixtures, and specially created graphics and decorations were used on this property. The octagonal-shaped produce stands are set out on a gray and white marble checkerboard patterned floor. A colorful frieze of giant scaled fruit and vegetable images cover the seven foot fascia that encompasses the department. These graphics "add a lively ambiance that reaches out to the shoppers in the market." Within the shelved wall units, the fruits and vegetables are artfully arranged in wire frame baskets. An angled mirror, below the cornice of the gondola that holds the fluorescent lamp, shows off the produce on the top shelf to the shopper standing in front.

Above left: The produce area with free-standing octagonal stands illuminated from above and the colorful graphic frieze.
Right: A close-up view of the wall fixture featuring the angled mirror and the baskets.
Photography: Rasheed Babu and Adnan Juneid.

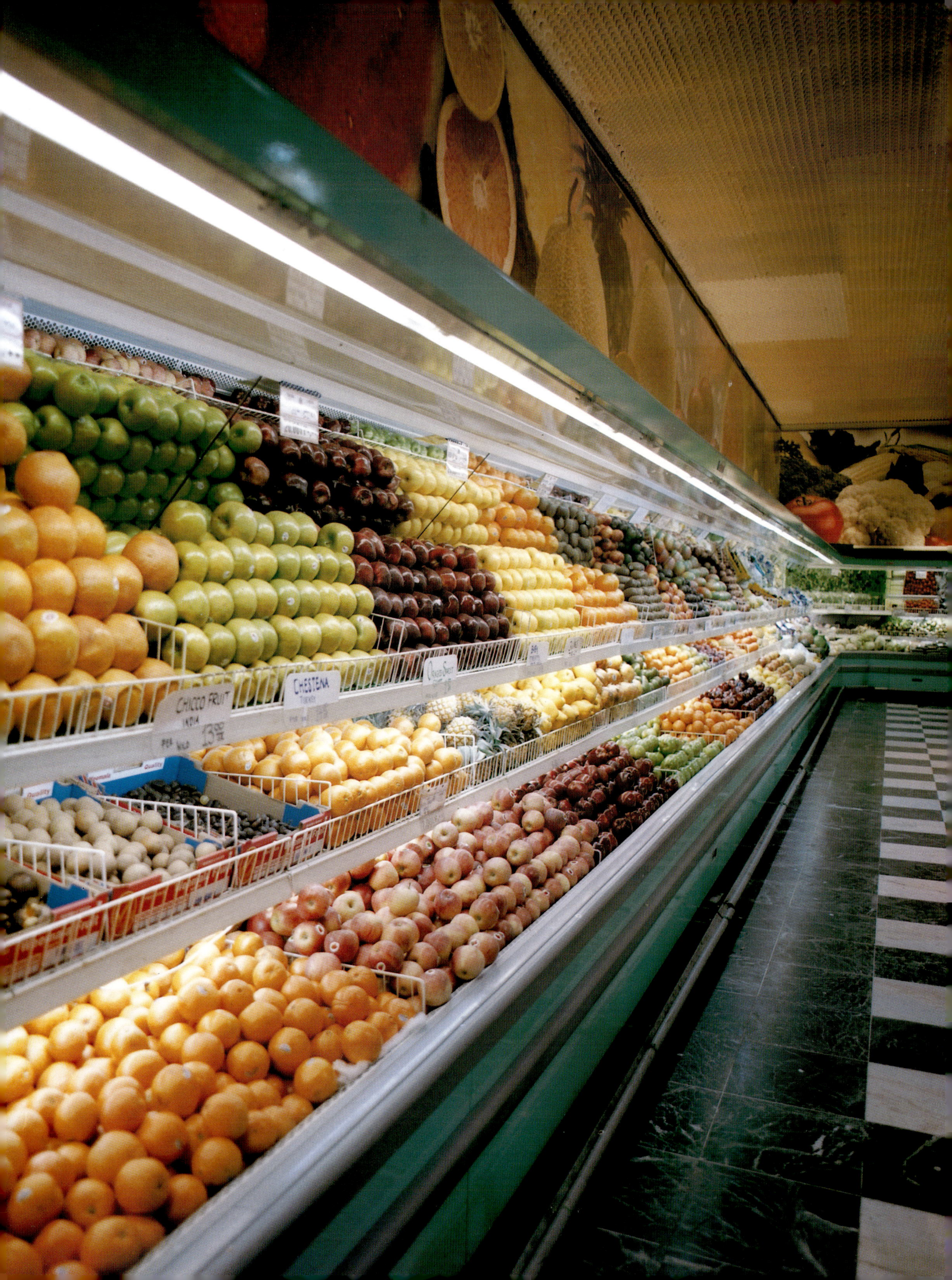
CHICCO FRUIT
INDIA
CHESTENA

Rich, deep natural woods, brass and terra cotta colored marble define the meat area. The refrigerated case is finished in a burl wood laminate accented with insets of brass just as the marble floor is highlighted with brass and black medallions. Antiqued brass finish pendant lights are suspended over the self illuminated cases and the warm light enriches the color of the meats on display. "MEAT"—written out in several languages and scripts—appears in gold and pewter on the creamy background walls. A gracious touch here is a pair of armchairs resting on small oriental style rugs accompanied by small tables affording the waiting customer a greater degree of comfort and a feeling of special service. The overhead sign says fresh salads and the metallic gold case, sitting on a white marble tile floor, is filled with assorted fresh vegetables all cut up and prepared "to go." This case makes a bold statement in the produce area-just beyond-which is defined by the black and white checkered marble floor.

Above: The cheese area is a sleek oval-shaped counter finished in white and decorated with rings of light around the columns in the corners.
Left: The fresh salad bar.
Opposite: The elegant meat boutique creates a feeling of quality, special service and customer attention.

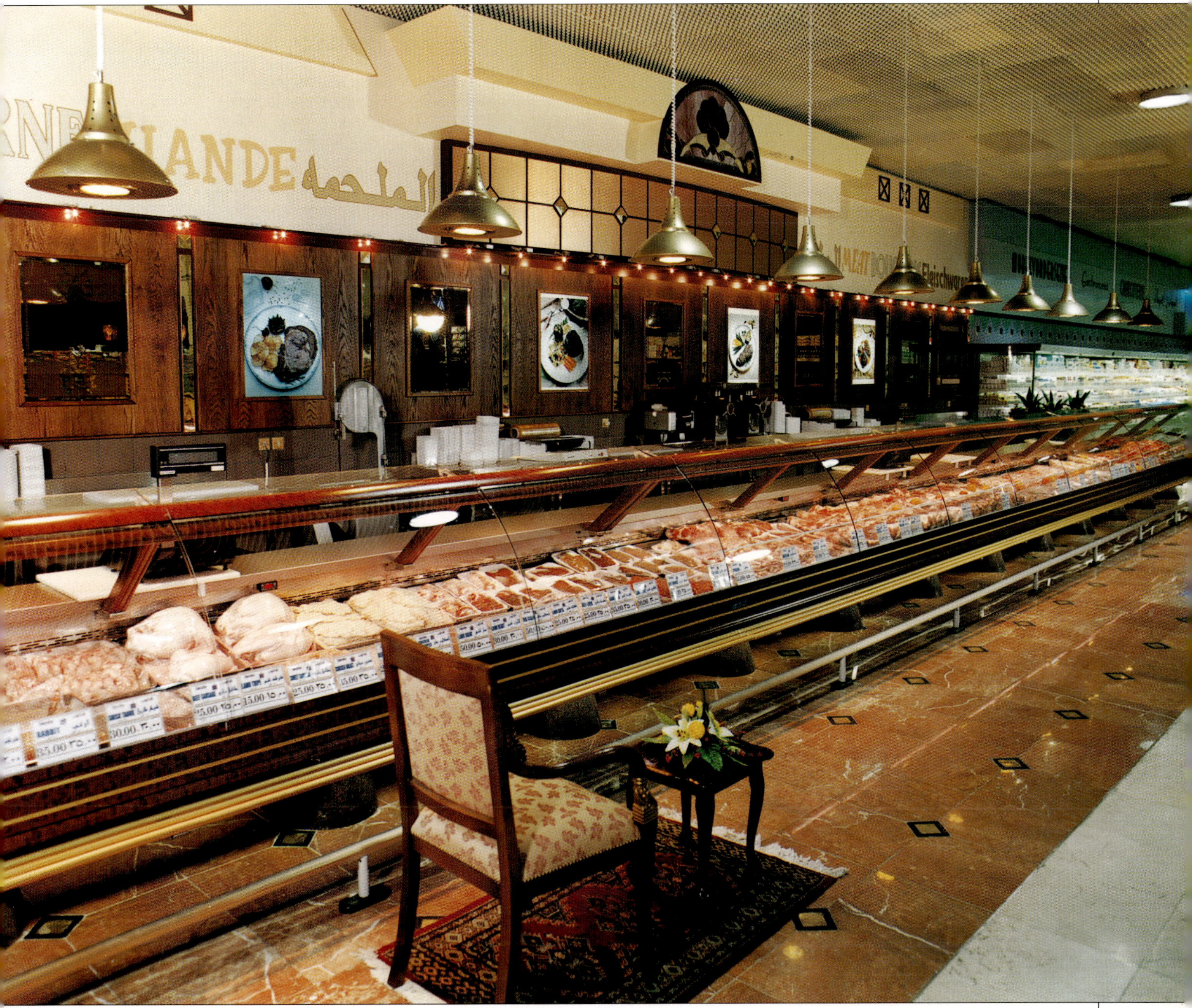
الملحمة

Danube Company Ltd.
Designed by
Mohammed Y. Al-Hasan

Danube Supermarket 4 Nahda
Jeddah, Saudi Arabia

Above: Globe lights attached to curved metal arms become light trees at the cheese counter.
Opposite: The fresh salad bar in the Heraa St. Supermarket.
Photography: Rasheed Babu and Adnan Juneid.

In the up and developing Nahda district where the Jeddah Hilton and Westin Hotel-Jeddah stand, Danube Supermarkets opened a 45,200 sq. ft. (4200 sq.m.) market. With the increased demand for better equipped and more comfortable "one-stop" shopping centers, the Danube Co. has evolved a design theory that calls for surrounding the supermarket with non-competitive retail stores and popular restaurants. In keeping with this idea, the designers work with hangar-type buildings that are void of supporting columns and that afford shoppers a feeling of openness and airiness. To please local tastes and to be true to the Arabic culture—expressed in modern architectural terms—the walls and side posts are painted with bright colors and decorated with geometric and/or flowing patterns to "provide a cheerful setting" for the food products on display. As shown here, colorful photo blow-ups of the many foods, housewares and home products found in the supermarket are used to add color and excitement to the space. Note the native decorative artwork on the angled piers between the photographic panels.

53

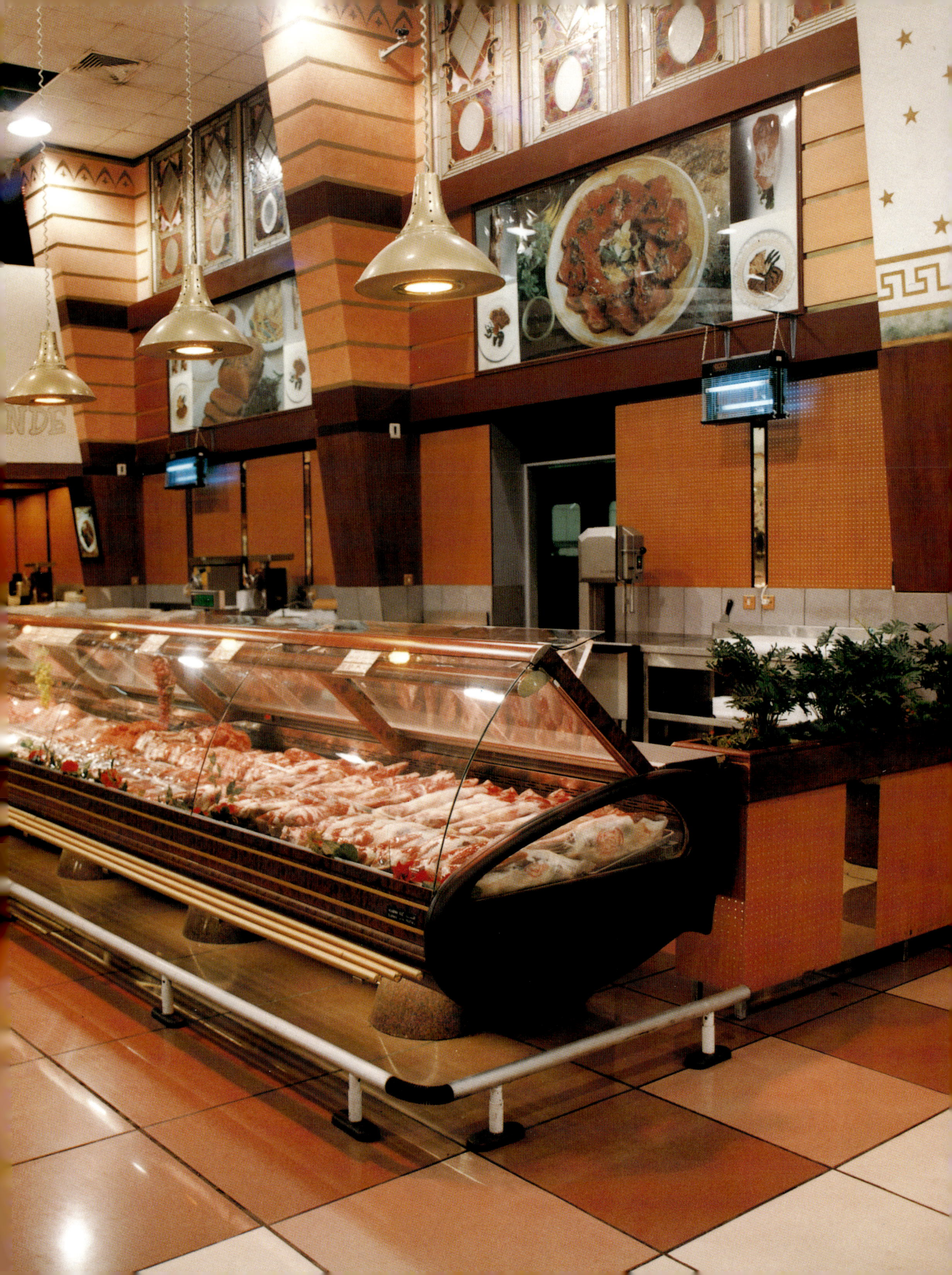

In the meat department the overall color feeling is warm, rich and earthy. Warm toast, terra cotta and pale salmon oversized ceramic tiles are decoratively patterned in front of the dark brown and brass trimmed refrigerator case. Perforated panels of an orange-toned wood are used on the back wall of the area and for the decorative planter. The same palette of colors used on the floor appears on the upper back wall—over the enlarged photos of the meat products. Native Arabic ceramic panels are set in the uppermost tier and here the angled piers are decorated with horizontal bands of the terra cotta and salmon colors. Adding to the fresh color of the meats are the hanging brass fixtures fitted with incandescent lamps. Throughout, the designers have humanized the scale and look of the supermarket with the stenciled artwork on the angled piers that break up the long perimeter walls into easily shopped sectors. The pastel colors and the light touch of the artwork is a pleasant relief from the extra high ceilings and wide open space.

Opposite: The meat area enriched with Arabic ceramic panels and an earthy palette of beige, salmon and terra cotta.

Above: The produce area and the deftly painted piers that break up the long walls.
Below: The cheese counter. Note the effective use of the globe-lit trees of light to highlight the counters and the product display.

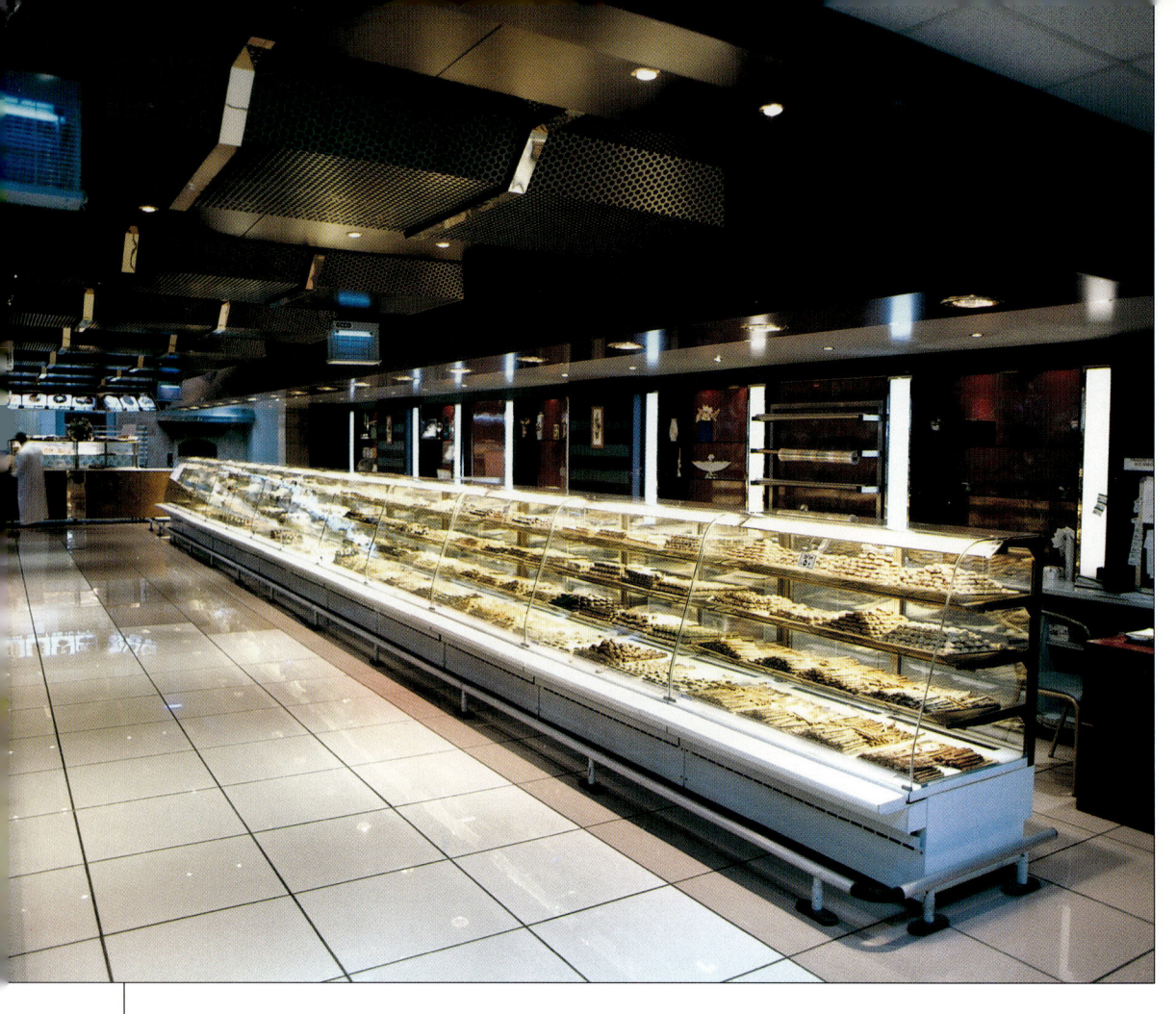

Above: Overall view of bakery department.

Not only does the aroma of the freshly-baked cookies, cakes and pastries draw customers to this bakery area but there is also an entertainment factor. Shoppers are invited to watch the bakers in this department as they work in the prep area readying these special treats for the ovens. Located on one of the shorter walls of the market and set beneath a mezzanine, the lower ceiling creates a more intimate feeling. This, enhanced by the rich, dark burgundy color of the walls and the perforated metal angled sleeves covering the heating ducts that cross over the ceiling creating an undulating effect. To counteract the low ceiling, glowing white vertical tubes of light pattern the rear wall create a series of bays or alcoves. Some have glass display shelves and others support the rolls of fancy wrapping paper used to prepare attractive gift platters of cookies and pastries. In addition to food products, Danube Supermarkets also include cafés, housewares and hardware areas, stationery and magazine shops as well as stations where film can be processed and printed.

Design Fabrications, Inc.

32400 Industrial Drive
Madison Heights
Michigan 48071
248.597.0988
248.597.0989 (Fax)
www.dfidesign.com
inquiries@dfidesign.com

Design Fabrications, Inc.

**Pick 'n Save
Zaneville, Ohio**

banners which are suspended overhead. In addition to depicting country market vignettes on the banners, others are interspersed that incorporate the store's logo.

Located alongside the Muskingum River in Ohio and servicing a small, working class community is the newly designed Pick"n"Save grocery store designed by Design Fabrications, Inc. The primary design objective was "to create an open market atmosphere while incorporating an industrial influence" into the 53,000 sq. ft. space. The free-standing store has two main entrances with ample parking in front. The commercial/industrial, split block, light gray building has a 22 ft. white, open deck ceiling which contributes to the open feeling within as do the white walls. Combined with the raw materials such as wood and metal, the interior envelop "lends focus to the graphics and architectural elements designed and produced by DFI. The main focus, upon entering, is the Fresh Market area. This centrally located space is pulled together by a multi-colored, grid-patterned floor of vinyl tiles and is accented by the brightly-colored

Top left: *The bold plaid of assorted colors and the colorful scenic banners set the scene for the Fresh Market.*

Above: *The glistening metal awning over the Fresh Choice area brings this shop into focus.*

58

The key ingredients of wood and metal introduced in the Fresh Market appear throughout the store. This is especially evident in the Meat department. Colorful floor tile patterns were created for both the meat and frozen food areas that also tie together each departments aisle cases. The designers specified stark white laminates and metal finishes for all the cases—to add to the clean and open feeling of the market. Banners featuring the store's logo lead the shopper down a path to the frozen food area where the "bold and fun hanging banners are suspended along the frozen food alley of cases. Included are unfinished galvanized fluorescent strip lighting above which ties into the steel industry theme" of the design. Large custom digital graphic vinyl wallcovering murals are used throughout the market to create "contrast and emphasis" while adding color to the otherwise neutral area. The wall murals in dairy and beverage are "eye-grabbers" and " create main focal points in each department." To help lead shoppers down the aisles there are custom aisle directories highlighted with bright colors, finished in maple veneer, and unfinished galvanized metal. 350-watt metal halide lighting is used in the main sales area to provide the general lighting while perimeter accent lighting accentuates the wall decor. "The shopping experience for this small community of shoppers is something all can relate to and feel welcome and invited, which provides for an enjoyable and exciting shopping excursion."

Left & below:
Throughout, the large digital graphics create a color contrast to the neutral space while creating focal emphasis for the various departments.

Photographer:
Michael Houghton Studio.

Design Fabrications, Inc.

Harmon's Market
Vandalia, Illinois

Left & below: Large, colorful wall murals, with raised lettering delineate the various "boutique" specialty areas.

For the rather intimate Harmon's Market in Vandalia, IL, DFI created a rather big shopping experience. Within the limited space of 32,000 sq. ft. the shopper will find—in addition to a wide selection of products—expanded deli and bakery areas as well as a café. "DFI worked to create a unique shopping environment through the use of graphics, lighting, and non-traditional 'boutique' department headings." The deli and bakery departments get the shoppers' attention at once. They are drawn to the large sandwich and cookie graphics over the unfinished, corrugated metal awning that highlights the shops. An expansive and colorful mural sweeps around the produce area to mark off the Berry Patch and Garden Spot zones and this mural, along with the aluminum silos and the dimensional lettering, define the department. To reinforce the outdoor market ambiance the sealed tan-colored concrete floor and the suspended canopies were added. The same tan floor is used in the check-out area while a concrete floor of another color appears in the main sales area. The "boutique" image continues in the dairy department—Hillside Creamery. Here a rural farm scene evokes the idea of "freshness and quality" as does the Udderly Delicious Milk mural on the adjacent wall. The old-fashioned Ice House with its brick vinyl wall covering, faux windows and corrugated metal overhang defines the frozen foods department.

The open joist ceiling, at 18 ft., changes from dark blue to light beige as the shopper enters the grocery area. The lighting also changes from the metal halide fixtures with high pressure sodium track lighting to suspended fluorescent strip fixtures. "The open joists, along with the light beige color help to reflect light, making the grocery area seem very open and airy, while providing the proper light levels required in the gondola areas." Throughout the market the individual departments are linked through the repetitive use of banners, the case colors and a burgundy stripe that runs around the perimeter of the store. The case colors are a constant neutral color accented with black bumpers and interiors which "create a nice contrast" for the merchandise displayed inside the cases. Hanging banners of the same shape direct shoppers from the deli and Bakery areas to the seven check-out lanes. Here, too, the same kind of banner is used to identify the lanes.

"Harmon's Market is sure to be a customer's first choice for shopping in Vandalia. The bright atmosphere along with the exciting images and signage make a person's shopping experience very enjoyable."

Above: Vinyl "brick" wallcovering and faux windows with corrugated metal awnings suggest an oudoor marketplace.

Below: Fun graphics and "boutique" signage create a special look for the dairy department.
Photography: Lew Portnoy.

Design Fabrications, Inc.

**Pick 'n Save River Edge
Wausau, Wisconsin**

The stand-alone, classic American Colonial-styled building that houses the Pick'N'Save market at the River's edge in Wausau, WI was designed to blend in and identify with the town's history and the local community. Finished in red brick, trimmed with cream dryvit and accented by mullioned windows, the 65,000 sq. ft. market has two entrances highlighted by the colonial-style porticos that allow shoppers to load and unload in comfort. "A primary design objective was to develop a sense of community and welcome customers into a time-remembered, 'taste-bud tempting' market." In addition, customers can enjoy views of the nearby river and conveniently park as they either shop or enjoy a snack or a meal in the café that is part of the market. The 22 ft., open deck ceiling adds to the open, spacious feeling of the space as do the many warm, natural textures used in the design. Though the Farmer's Market beckons shoppers upon entering the market, it is the aromas from the Red Rose Peddler—the flower shop—that really greets them and holds them. The Farmer's Market, true to the traditions of this Wisconsin community, suggests an old-fashioned, turn-of-the-previous century ambiance. The floors are laid with vinyl tiles that simulate wood and stone patterns to create a courtyard that reinforces the outdoors feeling. Aged, hand stenciled letters on the walls recall an old world setting as do the rustic shed awnings, the brick wall areas and the blow ups of antique food labels that now add accents of color. Bushels and baskets also contribute to the "fresh-from-the-farm" setting of this department. Mixed in with the enlarged food label illustrations are canvas banners with the store's corporate logo along with "rustic lettering" and "wave graphics" which together "help to define the individuality of this store."

Above left: The two portico entrances in the red brick, colonial-styled building.
Left: The Farmer's Market with the wood and stone simulated floor and the out-of-doors setting executed in faux brick and metal, and accented with the colorful banners.

The richly-colored banners repeat this personalized logo throughout the store. Directly opposite the Farmer's Market is the delicatessen and the hot foods area. Giant, dimensional foam graphics of the specific foods being offered are combined with a metal framework and awnings that extend out over the counters and cases. To set off the colorful graphics, panels of faux brick highlight the area and the previously-mentioned canvas banners add bright splashes of color. Rich wood textured laminates are used on the cases and counters and the walls are highlighted with hand painted ivy over rag-rolled surfaces. "The color palette evokes a warm, old time feeling with the use of earthy, rich tones accented with a bright golden hue for sparkle. The dark blue—nearly black—ceiling simulates a midnight sky which creates a more intimate space below and also promotes dramatic highlighting for trimming the tables of perishable goods below."

Above: The dimensional foam graphics and sign highlight the meats area.

Below: Corrugated metal, rough hewn wood, brick and hand painted lettering are used to create an old-times feeling for the up-to-date dairy & frozen foods areas.

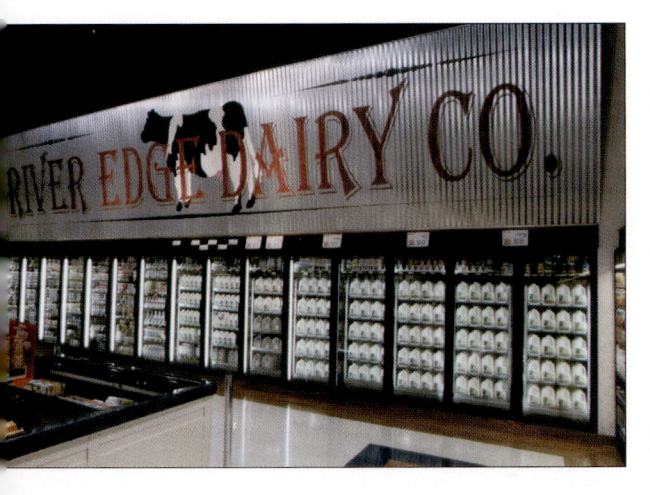

Left: The Main Street Market with its awnings and the checkerboard motif.
Above: The wrap-around fascia that highlights the Red Rose Peddler.
Below: The striking dimensional signage over The Cellar.

The Market Street Delicatessen is filled with good old-fashioned flavors. The checkerboard design of the vinyl floor in front of the display cases is repeated on the rear wall of the "shop" in ceramic tiles. The same motif can be seen on the fascia over the merchandise that follows. Colorful canvas awnings on metal frames extend over the cases and frame the dimensional sign that is easily seen and read from almost anywhere in the market. The use of dimensional foam sculptured elements combined with metal frames and cut-out letters can also be appreciated as together they make a dramatic entrance to The Cellar: the wine and liquor department. The Floral Department, previously mentioned, gains its visual prominence from the giant wrap-around fascia which is brightly painted with red roses and trailing vines and foliage. The bakery, like the meat area, is accentuated by the striped canvas awnings. The River Walk Café is adjacent to the delicatessen and provides a relaxing environment for the shopper as well as a view of the river. In order to create the overall desired lighting for the space, the designers had to come up with a lighting plan that combined excellent lighting with low maintenance. 350-watt metal halide fixtures were combined with lower level fluorescent fixtures for the general lighting. For the accent lighting to highlight the decorative elements, low maintenance, high pressure sodium track lighting was used. To add "warm sparkle to the product" PAR track and low voltage lamps were included. The island cases were illuminated from within. This not only emphasized the product display but "eliminated the line-of-sight problem caused by hanging linear fluorescents over the cases." "This grocery store offers the growing community a warm, sophisticated shopping atmosphere that enhances the total grocery shopping experience."

Above: The entrance to the River Walk Café and the bakery beyond.
Below: The 13 check-out lanes are defined by the illuminated space frames with planter boxes and the candy cane check-out lights.
Photography: Jeffery Davis.

Design Fabrications, Inc.

**Sunmart
Moorhead, Minnesota**

There is a fun feeling about shopping in the spacious, 50,000 sq. ft. Sunmart Market in Moorhead, MT. DFI matched the challenge of this expansive space with larger-than-life decor and bright colors—"adding fun and excitement to the shopping experience." As the shopper makes his or her way through the open space under the light colored, exposed ceiling, each of the individual areas or departments is accented by "large splashes of primary colors and food graphics." To unify the space and create an overall sense of ambiance, there are stylized storefronts which are created by soffit build-outs and the use of a brick wallcovering that was specially developed by DFI. To bring the imagery into scale for the shoppers, the canopies that front these "shops" have magnetic chalkboard fascias with interchangeable slogan magnets. To reinforce the Sunmart's commitment to quality and low prices, smaller institutional signs are strategically placed around the store. The apple logo, the company's identity, is also used as a recurring decorative motif. The decor scheme is enhanced by the colorful curved landscapes of Big Food Land and the oversized whimsical banners. Up front is The American Sandwich & Grill which features a cafeteria-style menu and a self-service drink bar. An adjacent 1950's themed café offers shoppers a place to take a break. A hanging space frame and large trellis-like sign identify the centrally located flower shop and pharmacy, health & beauty products and video rental departments are added attractions for the Sunmart shopper. A truly special treat is the Kids Korner located near

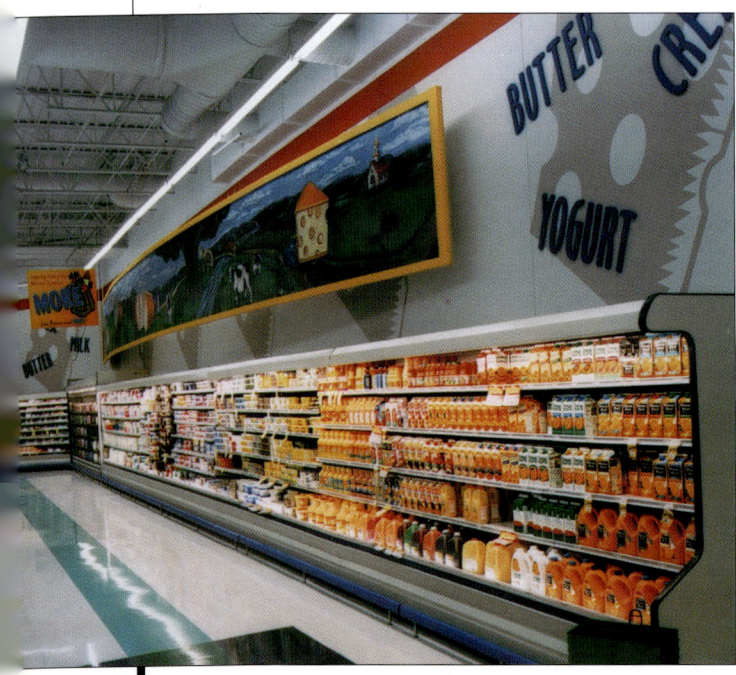

Above left: A typical shop front setting for the delicatessen which includes "brick" work, awnings and pseudo windows. The colorful overscaled graphic "sells and tells" the story.
Left: Curved murals of the farmlands identify the dairy department.

the check-out. The exterior is covered with amusing graphics and within there are toys, games and activities to keep the children happy—and safe behind the glass panels—while the parents are free to shop. "Sunmart provides the city of Moorhead with more than a grocery store by supporting an unlimited number of services in the store. Nash Finch, with the help of DFI, has successfully united these elements under one roof while entertaining the customers and adding 'big' excitement to the shopping experience."

Above: *The American Sandwich & Grill and Café are two of the popular "stops" along the market route.*
Left: *The fun shop front of the bakery and the glass enclosed play area for children: Kids Korner.*
Photography: *Hanson Photo Video Communication.*

Design Fabrications, Inc.

Pick 'n' Save
Mukwonago, Wisconsin

For almost a century the McAdams family has been associated with food service. With this store in Mukwonago, WI—where it all began—a new look is emerging. "History played an important role when it came to remodeling this location." It became a nostalgic trip in all new surroundings. The service meat department, for example, is identified above a canvas awning as The McAdams Butcher Shop. A replica of the sign used back in the 1930's hangs here as well as chalkboards with weekly specials. "This pays homage to the founder of the Palace Meat Market whose legacy still lives on under the name Pick 'n' Save."

Right: One of the two farm and orchard murals in the produce area. They are framed by face brick pilasters.
Photography: Edward Purcell.

DFI worked to create a comfortable shopping environment through the use of large, billboard-style graphics, exterior style canopies, and face brick pilasters. In the produce department, the standing seam metal canopies are framed by brick pilasters and faux windows which create an out-of-doors, roadside farm setting. Adding to the nostalgia are the large sepia prints of vintage historical sites. Hot foods, deli and bakery departments move into the main service area and are identified by softer, custom-screened canvas awnings. The words "neighborhood" and "corner" evoke a sense of welcome and old-time friendly service. The cherry colored wood floors help to "depict a natural, wholesome environment" for the natural foods department. The navy blue color visually lowers the ceiling to create a more intimate setting. The burgundy crown molding provides a transition from the ceiling to the wall murals and the wall surfaces that have been "aged" by means of a rag rolled paint technique. The large scale billboard murals continue around the perimeter walls, and are complemented by the brick pilasters and the faux windows. Metal halide fixtures provide the general illumination. The billboards are highlighted by fluorescent wall wash fixtures. As the shopper passes through the checkout lane he/she sees "Thank You! The McAdams Family." It reminds him/her of the history associated with the store and company.

Above: The coffee boutique is presented between brick pilasters with wood-toned vinyl floor.
Upper right: A canvas canopy extends off the wall in hot foods. Faux windows suggest the out-of-doors ambiance.
Lower right: Fluorescent wall washers highlight billboard-style murals. Metal halides provide general illumination.

Design Fabrications, Inc.

Steele's Market
Fort Collins, Colorado

The brick and stone, contemporary building that houses Steele's Market anchors a small shopping center. The modern design which is detailed with architectural steel elements is not only community based in its design concept but is part of the community pavilion which includes parking, pedestrian walk-ways, extensive landscaping and ornamental light fixtures. This 62,000 sq. ft. project was a team effort. DFI designed the graphics, signage & canopies and interior were designed by Neenan Archistruction and Architect Greg D. Fisher. The idea was to affect a setting that would tie in with the community's agricultural and historical roots—but done in a contemporary manner."
"Traditional exterior materials, along with historical black and white photographs and replica windmills help to depict the lifestyle of a byegone era." This design concept comes together on the Welcoming Wall—up front—which separates the produce department from the health & beauty area. The combination of corrugated metal, birch plywood and painted vinyl siding—in a variety of shapes, sizes and textures—is an indication of what is still to come. Galvanized metal panels serve as backgrounds for the applied departmental sign letters. In the produce area the stained concrete floor represents the earth or the ground which is the usual floor covering of outdoor farmers' markets. The fabric canopies that are suspended over the tables set out in the middle of the floor are reminiscent of the old-fashioned farm stand awnings. The rows of tented awnings that not only add a dash of color to the area, also support the spot downlights that accentuate the rich colors of the assorted fruits and vegetables.

Mixed in between the sleek contemporary floor units in produce are the rustic wood farm crates and even some specialty cart displayers on big casters that add the farm-fresh feeling of a farm roadside stand to this area. The corrugated panels that were introduced up front also appear as abstract farm silos towering over the wall display of produce. Leading to other areas of the market are the assorted colors and patterns of vinyl tiles on the floors. There are areas of solid colors laid in bold geometric designs, diagonally striped areas and oversized checkerboard patterns as in the dairy and grocery areas. In addition to a "new environment" the designers have added some new features such as wider aisles in the grocery area which not only makes it easier for the shopper but more comfortable as well. "This allows customers to spend more time looking at products and still allow room for other shoppers (and their carts) to get by." The deli also has been expanded to include an extensive home meal replacement center where professional chefs prepare the "take-out" meals for the "time-starved customers".

Far left: *The produce area is defined by the tent-top awnings that bring attention to the products on the polished, "earthy" concrete floor.*
Below: *Other views of the produce department and the adjacent specialty shops.*

Left: The galvanized metal band runs along the wall in dairy. Decorative farm-like props are arranged over the product display to affect an "old" look in a "new" setting.
Below: The cinder block wall of frozen foods is seen on the rear wall-behind the grocery gondolas. Silos are suggested by the use of the corrugated metal panels on the perimeter walls.
Photography: La Casse Photography.

The perimeter walls of the store are yet another "contemporary interpretation of agricultural elements." Thin metal channels separate the clear coated birch panels that are used to sheath the expanded deli department. The prep walls get a great visual lift—and a little glimmer—from the galvanized metal with a quilted diamond pattern. The metal is not only an effective alternative to the ceramic tiles usually used but it "helps to keep with the architectural theme." A band of corrugated metal—a recurring material motif—runs along the rear of the store "suggesting the textures of a silo." To simulate concrete or cinder blocks, the gray wall of the frozen foods area is patterned with an oversized brick design created by strips of angled aluminum. The old/new theme has succeeded admirably in this Steele's Market. "With all the new features as well as an opportunity to catch glimpses of the past, Steele's Market is certainly a desirable shopping destination for residents of Fort Collins and surrounding areas."

Heights Venture Architects, LLP

1111 North Loop West
Suite 800
Houston
Texas 77008
713.869.1103
713.869.5573 (Fax)
stephen.jovicich@hva.cc
www.hva.cc

4801 Arapaho
Suite 200
Addison
Texas 75001
972.490.7292
972.490.7444 (Fax)
robert.holton@hva.cc
www.hva.cc

Heights Venture Architects, LLP

**Flagship concept
Randalls # 64 Bellaire, Texas
Randalls # 11 Houston, Texas**

Left: 50's era exterior facade before remodel.
Below left: New vestibule structure and landscape echo new interior changes. Prominent brick masonry façade connotes permanence and increases visibility from street.
Below: Wine department.
Photography: Rex Spencer.

Food store designs evolve over time to meet the ever changing needs of the clients, shoppers, and community at large as was the case with these two existing stores. The neighborhood demographic changed dramatically into an upscale client base seeking a broader selection of foods, wines, and service. The initial Flagship concept developed several years before by Brown/Bunyan/Moon/ and More and Heights Venture offered the upscale décor suitable for this community but the design was too elaborate for the existing structure and too costly a design to be justifiable. The Randalls store serving Bellaire Texas (#64) offered a prime opportunity to explore how the Flagship concept could be applied to a smaller footprint (32,340 gsf) without sacrificing the upscale elegance and high level of service associated with the chains' flagship stores. Site restraints precluded expanding the store but careful fixture and operations planning allowed kitchen size and warehouse space to be reduced. Sales area went from 22,065 to 26,077 sf, allowing for greater variety of offerings and an expanded wine room. Reflective metallic ceiling and floor tiles replicating dark green marble, coupled with wood cabinetry, create a sense of a traditional wine cellar. MR16 spot lighting along the ceiling and on the cabinet valence displays the wines clearly while enhancing and warming the space. Service departments were illuminated with prismatic glass liners modified to serve as chandeliers providing clear warm light wherever service is available. Perimeter cove lighting establishes a bright line as a visual reference and a data line from which the graphics suspend. HVA teamed with Douglas/Gallagher to develop a simple but elegant graphic package. Primary graphics, identifying services offered, became illuminated etched glass signage eliminating excessive levels of décor and details. An uncomplicated floor pattern was used throughout the sales area changing only at the wine cellar and power alley. Flooring in the power alley consists of vinyl strips which mimic the appearance of solid oak flooring conjuring the warmth of the corner deli or bakery from by-gone eras. A new exterior vestibule, covered canopies, and new landscaping significantly improve the visibility and appearance of the store establishing it as a true neighborhood center.

Top right: Bakery and deli.
Right: Meat and seafood department.
Below right: Perimeter aisle.

Top left: Old lodge form building shell lacked presence in an upscale neighborhood on the cusp of revitalization.

Top right: New exterior protected vestibule provides for covered carts returning interior floor sales area.

Below: View across cheese island, full service deli provides robust selection of prepared foods for view and maintains close connection to customer.

Right: *Floral department creates a colorful and festive entry.*
Center: *Produce department. Black interior lining in wall cases forces the eye to see the product within.*
Bottom: *Off-the-path wine department invites customer to consider the evening's selection.*

The existing Randalls store (#11) serving several west Houston neighborhoods had enjoyed an upper income clientele for many years but the merchandising plan and décor elements were not meeting all of the services being offered. Once again, Heights Venture, working in close collaboration with Randalls management rose to the occasion to reorganize the various departments, add sales space, and update the décor package to reflect a simple elegance and clarity of space. The exterior underwent a dramatic change from a lodge style structure and frame to a traditional post modern expression reflecting the changes within. The new vestibule towers offered improved protection from the elements and protected cart storage adding sales and circulation area to the interior. Main identity graphics were redesigned in cooperation with Douglas/Gallagher to provide a clear visual reference without the expense of the etched glass graphic used before in Bellaire. Kitchen wall tiles and accents were simplified to promote a clean and bright area which did not take attention away from the product. New vinyl wood flooring was installed over much of the existing quarry tile in the power alley to reduce basket noise yet maintain the polished interior presentation a high service customer had come to expect. Color corrected spot lighting was added throughout the power alley to highlight the product and highlight the colors of the fresh produce.

Heights Venture Architects, LLP

Flexible concept
Randalls # 480 Austin, Texas

Left: Exterior view. Spanish colonial detailing of entire shopping center responds to the hill country's mixed architectural heritage.
Below left: Front service aisle creates an outdoor arcade experience. Customer service counter becomes part of the shopping experience between the video entertainment center and the one hour photo store.
Photography: Rex Spencer.

Randalls Food and Drugs charged Heights Venture with the task of developing the concept of a European Market to meet their specific needs and operations. The idea of an indoor market place had seen several iterations overseas based on design parameters established by P.K. Halstead. Working with the design team from PK Halstead to establish merchandise and operations goals, HVA developed a radical new design which set a new bar for operational flexibility. The Spanish colonial exterior of the store and shopping center belies the design and high tech flexibility developed for the interior. Heights Venture again retained Douglas/Gallagher to develop a new graphics concept with the same flexibility offered by the market design. The additional challenge was to carry the details and materials of the graphics from primary to secondary to tertiary signage, including the pricing labels. Excepting the sales gondolas, the entire interior space was equipped with a bus bar power delivery system from Lite-Lab which powered all lights and equipment for the various departments. The grid established a floating plane and organizing element for the space. Extensive use of self contained refrigerated display cases allowed the ultimate in flexibility and seasonal adaptation.

Right: The ultimate in flexibility. Furrdown, ceiling, fluorescent fixtures, lights, graphics, and equipment are all hung from and powered by LiteLab busway system. (Photo courtesy of LiteLab).

Below: View across the power alley featuring the produce preparation area where patrons and staff can interact. Special requests can be honored. (photo courtesy of Litelab)

79

Above: Wine department. Lighting bridge yields infinite options in configuring display lighting.
Right: Sales aisles feature warehouse shelving lends atmosphere and expands available storage. Valence lighting minimizes tunnel effect and highlights the merchandise.

Entire departments could be reconfigured or relocated in a matter of hours by staff. Décor elements necessarily had to enjoy the same flexibility. Ceilings, light fixtures, furrdowns, and graphics for the covered food prep areas were detailed to suspend from the same power grid. Light was brought down to the merchandise and put into valence lighting at the gondolas or spotted onto the merchandise from the grid using theatre style light fixtures. Warehouse style gondolas add to the atmosphere one expects in an open market environment and adds significant storage capability to the store.

The front service aisle was designed to illicit an outdoor arcade experience drawing the customer into the video and photo areas with bright colors and illuminated signage. Neon main identity graphics and banners alone float free above the power grid always providing a visual reference above the grid for the shopper to find their way. Stained, scored, and polished concrete flooring continued throughout the store, tying the floor plane into one unified and integrated whole. The results were dramatic and continued to enjoy a positive response from new store customers. Ultimately, only two of these projects were completed as several of early design concerns became manifest in the operations: so much self contained equipment raised noise and heat levels within the sales area and the store held a greater flexibility for change than was truly needed.

Above: *Endcap sales are featured by the use of theatre light fixtures.*
Left: *Floral department. Features a walk through all glass floral cooler. Greeting card display in close proximity.*

Heights Venture Architects, LLP

New Generation Prototype Design

Left: *Overhead busway provides flexibility in locating refrigerated or heated display cases for maximum effect and seasonal needs.*
Below: *Clean open views and triangular aisle markers allow customers to locate goods they seek.*
Photography:
Rex Spencer.

The New Generation food store prototype resulted from the lessons learned in developing the flexible concept and many stores classed as New Generation concepts. Although the Flexible Market concept enjoyed great success, emphasis changed to develop an interior design which was "clean and bright". Additionally, Randalls outlined an aggressive expansion campaign which could only be met in the design and development of a truly prototypical foodstore design. The Heights Venture store planning team, in close collaboration with the Randalls corporate management laid out a true prototype. The plan allowed the flexibility to adjust specific cases to meet local demographics and seasonal adjustments as well as providing the efficiency of a true prototype. The same basic plan and interior design was then duplicated in over twenty new stores built within a three year period. The "Market" feel was retained in planning the power alley. The overhead grid was reduced but continued to offer the flexibility to move powered displays and lighting without special construction trades. Theatre lighting remained integral in highlighting the product. Interior finish materials were kept in the neutral ranges and clean patterns to keep the attention on merchandise and not on the facility. Copper awnings completely ring the perimeter breaking only for billboard graphics which mark the various departments and entrances. The perimeter awnings allowed the lighting to be brought down to the product and served to establish a human scale at wall cases and in the service areas creating a more intimate space. Primary, secondary, and tertiary graphics were a continued evolution of those developed in earlier New Generation stores and refined in the Flexible concept stores. Heights Venture continued collaboration with Douglas/Gallagher

Top left: Copper awnings completely ring the perimeter breaking only for billboard graphics to mark a department or entrance.
Above: Bakery.
Below: Primary and secondary graphics clearly indicate merchandise along a continuous bank of service cases.

Above: Billboard graphics call attention to the various specialty shops and departments.
Below: Service counters on every side of the power alley increase connection of customer to service staff. Careful placement and screening of fluorescent lighting maintain control of stage lighting of fresh products.

to adapt the graphics program to offer a consistent graphic message all the way down to the package labels on the products. Three sided aisle markers were designed to provide the maximum visibility, allowing a shopper to find the merchandise they desire from almost any point in the store. Extensive décor elements and overly complex motifs were avoided in establishing the design. A well articulated and informed design keeps the focus on the product and not on the surroundings. The New Generation prototype has proven to meet Randalls needs by meeting the needs of the customer.

Left: View down power alley.
Below: Color corrected high pressure sodium theatre lighting throughout the power alley highlights the merchandise not the building.

Heights Venture Architects, LLP

New Generation Exterior Options

Different communities have different needs which can often cause problems in meeting an aggressive building program. Many municipalities and new developments are now establishing rigid criteria to control the overall appearance of their communities and ensure their long term viability. Heights Venture's extensive experience in the design and development of shopping centers proved its value in developing an array of exterior options from which to select. Overall site conditions, climate, regulatory restrictions and local demographics were considered in selecting the exterior option to be used with adaptations made for site specific requirements and finishes. The shell designs typically incorporated a large conditioned vestibule with side entrances on either side of the vestibule. Each side entry hosted a generous open air porch which not only allowed ample protection from bad weather but served as sales areas to merchandise floral and gardening merchandise. The large central mass of the vestibule increased visibility and provided a large canvas for a generous store sign.

Top: Night view of Tom Thumb # 574 – Fort Worth, Texas.
Left: Randalls # 71 Pearland, Texas - An extremely popular design with developers and Randalls this prototype design was implemented in over a dozen locations.
Photography: Rex Spencer.

Left: Randalls # 1774 – Houston, Texas.
Below: Randalls # 1778 Austin, Texas.

Heights Venture Architects, LLP

Next Generation Prototypical Shell Designs

Top left: 1896 Cedar Park, Texas. Increasing the color range of the cast stone and roof tile allows this project to fit into the hill country vernacular.
Below: 1972 Mansfield, Texas. Scale and range of the ashlar cast stone allow the entrances to stand out in sharp contrast. Eyebrow metal canopy protects customers from rain and controls solar exposure in the vestibule.

Top right: 1858 Pearland, Texas. Deep burgundy brick makes a bold statement.
Below right: 1925 Rowlett, Texas. Light colored cast stone, brick and trim.
Photography: Rex Spencer.

New corporate criteria, sales, and design needs were brought to the Randalls & TomThumb food store chain with their acquisition by Safeway. New stores were to use the plans developed by the corporate design team and incorporate a crisp and colorful "Marquee Décor" interior package developed by King Design International. Heights Venture developed several exterior options adapted specifically for this store prototype in order to support their building program. Experience had shown that for a building program to be efficient and effective, the exterior design must be able to be replicated in many different municipalities and be adapted to meet the local vernacular. Massing, circulation, and suitability for climate are key. Once these components are correctly designed, finish materials and details can readily be adjusted to meet almost any developer or code review. A building's visual mass can be controlled through the selection of colors and textures. Large, bold, stone or brick finishes add prominence and appear larger than the same entrance treated with smooth plaster finishes and a neutral palette.

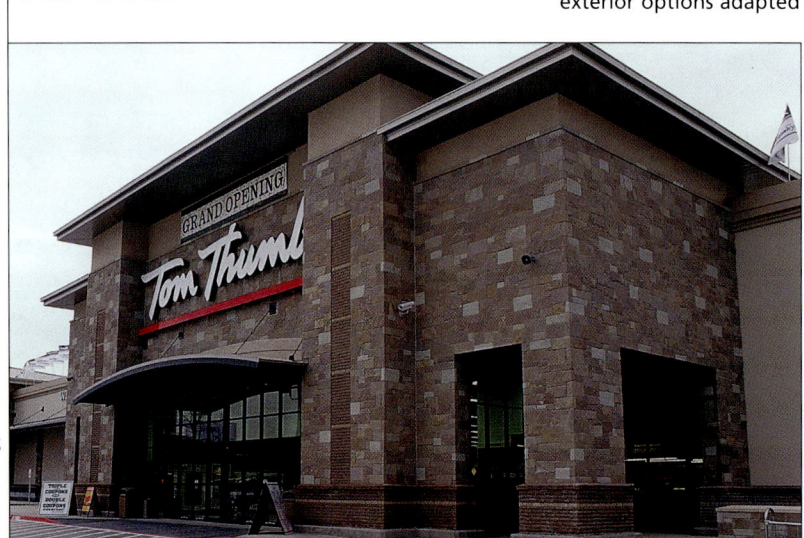

King Design International

3850 W. First Avenue
Eugene
Oregon 97402
800.533.2796
541.686.2848
541.686.8418 (Fax)
marketing@kingdesign.com
www.kingdesign.com

King Design International

Gelson's
Pasadena, California

"It's not creative unless it translates to the real world—and works!" With that credo foremost in mind, King Design International, the designers of Gelson's 25,000 sq. ft. Pasadena store, combined a Southern California art deco sensitivity with the successful presentation of produce and food products. Three entrances, one from the lower lobby to the underground parking, lead into the space where the ceilings vary from 11 to 14 ft. The challenging footprint is narrow and deep—with a dog leg extension—and with structural columns that created design problems. By using floating ceilings, and adding architectural features and murals to the columns, the designers were able to satisfactorily incorporate the merchandise layout provided by the client. The client requested that the interior design tie-in with the local community and have an upscale look. The designers satisfied these objectives with the use of deco colored laminates and paints, ceramic tiles and a variety of finishes. To add to the "look," special departmental signage—unique and individualized for each department—and architectural features and graphics all in the art deco style, defined each space and product line. The custom chandeliers over the entrance, check-out and service areas and the fireside seating also add to this delightful ambiance. To quote the designers, "We were very successful in minimizing the architectural challenges. We, and the client, were very pleased with the results. The store is dramatic and creates a great shopping experience for the customer."

Opposite left: The customer service desk features one of KDI's creative signs.
Left: The dramatically decorated dropped ceiling over produce.
Above right: A Southern California/art deco feeling permeates the total design.
Right: Views of several of the special departmental signs.
Photography: King Design International.

King Design International

**Safeway Inc.
USA and Canada**

Safeway, Inc. a chain of supermarkets in the USA and Canada, wanted to improve and upscale their corporate appearance and have a design that "created a warm and comfortable atmosphere for the shopper." The challenge for KDI was to create a prototype design that was not only distinctive and adaptable but could be implemented throughout the chain within a set budget. The design had to look good in a variety of locations, layouts and formats and combine with a branding concept evolved by a marketing company to create "a more unified corporate look." To accomplish this we (KDI) concentrated on designing elements that were visually complicated but easy to install." The

Above left: Dark purple and textured ivory, framed in teak, appear on the cornices over the perimeter departments.
Left: The florist shop sits on an overscaled grid of terrazzo-like vinyl and is identified by the large flower logos.
Photography: King Design International (above left); Long's Photography (left).

design included deeper and richer colors. These colors which varied from department to department were combined with a basic "Sagewood" Nevamar laminate. Purple, textured ivory and gold vinyls cover the walls and are trimmed with teak and accented in black. The lower walls are covered in Marlite's teak or "olive fog" paint. Banners create an easy way for shoppers to distinguish the location of departments and the wall graphics and copy are large enough and easy to read throughout the space. Copy and graphic ovals are departmentalized with color. The designers state, "The color scheme and finishes add variety, warmth and interest—more of a small chain approach than a large chain and the signage and graphics become a cohesive, well received package."

Above and right: Examples of the departmental signage by KDI that created the "cohesive, well received package" for Safeway.
Photography: King Design International (right); Long's Photography (above, upper right, middle right).

King Design International

Jensen's Finest Foods
La Quinta, California

The 13,000 sq. ft. Jensen's Finest Foods market blends with the Southern California setting and the La Quinta community with its contemporary desert tones on stucco, the soft shapes, flat roof and pueblo-style facade. There is even a trellis for sun control over outdoor seating. The answer to the client's request for "a very upscale, architectural design that focused the attention on the merchandise," KDI created a space that is unique and different. The special materials and details such as the flagstone, the chandeliers for dramatic lighting, the back-lit translucent panels on the upper perimeter walls and the blend of "old world" and contemporary styles make this Jensen's outstanding. The unusual store layout is on a diagonal. As schemed by KDI it easily guides the shopper through the 18 ft. high space where the open truss ceiling is painted dark brown. The angles "create interesting areas for merchandising not found in typical stores." In keeping with the contemporary look, simple brushed turquoise steel faced copy was used and back-lit for extra emphasis and readability in the store. With a creative combination of visual merchandising, fixturing and lighting KDI can generate the kind of excitement that transforms everyday shopping into an enjoyable experience. Jensen's Finest Foods is the proof.

Above: Unexpected angles and changing flooring materials add to the visual excitement of the project.
Photography: King Design International.

Below: Flagstone combined with sandstone vinyl flooring material on the walls, and deep teak on the floor create the setting for the floral area.

Above: The deep brown ceiling supports the chandeliers that distinguish the main entrance. The wine/liquor area is in the rear.
Right: From the checkout to the deli/bakery, the white gloss tile and pewter trim delineate the service departments.

King Design International

Nob Hill Foods
Part of the Raley's Family of Fine Stores
Salinas, California

Give us a "light and bright store with a fresh color palette" was the main request from the client for the interior design package of the Nob Hill #630, 45,000 sq. ft. free-standing store in Salinas, CA. Says King Design International, "We were successful in designing a decor package that highlighted the surrounding agricultural and farming community, while at the same time providing a clean, contemporary and bright interior for the shoppers. This décor package was a successful prototype to help this chain reinvent itself in creating a more contemporary setting without losing the neighborhood feeling." To accomplish this, KDI used light colored materials and paints accented with deeper colors for interest and custom designed wall murals to relate more closely with local scenery and products. These murals not only created "warm comfortable backgrounds" for the perimeter departments, but made them more visual for shoppers in this traditionally laid out market. The color palette consists mainly of creams, various tones of peach and mossy green, accented with dark green, and maple woods. The maple wood appears as a laminate on fixtures and is accented with simulated slate. The 16 ft. ceiling is finished with T-bar and acoustical tiles and the lighting plan combines recessed fluorescent lamps for the main sales area and decorative pendants in the service departments. Track lighting is incorporated for highlighting products and artwork. Illuminated dropped ceilings in meat, seafood, deli and bakery add "unexpected" touches as does the trellis treatment. This design package can be readily adapted to the local flavor of future stores in this chain.

Above left and left:
The unusual trellis over the bakery complements the curved trellis that surrounds the meats/seafood service area shown just below. Maple wood trim adds to the feeling of wholesomeness and naturalness of the products. Delicatessen is on the right.
Photography: Long's Photography.

Delicatessen

"It's good food and not fine words that keeps me alive" - Moliere

This page: The custom mural, in produce, extends across the department and highlights typical scenes of the Salinas Valley. Special lighting fixtures highlight the produce bins.

King Design International

**Thrifty Foods
Tsawwassen
Delta, British Columbia, Canada**

Above: The Farmer's Market ambiance is created in produce with the use of metal siding and brick wall treatments.
Below: The curved metal canopy and natural textures further enhance the outdoors feeling in produce.
Photography: King Design International.

In the Thrifty Foods market shown here, the client got more than was expected from the design package created by KDI. This 21,000 sq. ft. sales area with open truss and peaked ceilings that go from 10 to 16 ft., is more than just "an open market feeling with individualized departments"—as requested by the client. It is the essence of the Northwest community captured and reinterpreted in a contemporary vernacular for the local citizens. The wide use of cedar, timber and local rock and stone combined with vinyl slate, board and batten, faux rocks and heavily textured wall coverings create the desired ambiance. Cedar and slate laminates cover many of the counters and cases. To not break from the out-of-doors, Northwest illusion, some faux stone and timber beam work has been integrated into the lighting fixtures. In some instances, the ceiling is open to the deck. In other areas, the ceiling is dropped. A stained glass, faux skylight gives prominence to the produce display, while the vaulted peaked ceilings at the two entrances are visual highlights. To accentuate the custom illustrat-

This page: Simulated building facades, rich in texture, continue the feeling of an out-of-doors marketplace where the individual shops are "housed" at street level.

ed murals, spots are used as well as on the product displays. Decorative pendants hang in the service areas. Says KDI of their association with this client, "Our designs really work well when we get good direction, and lots of latitude from the client. This is a perfect example of that collaboration."

King Design International

Market of Choice
Ashland, Oregon

Ashland, OR is home to the Oregon Shakespeare Festival. This 14,000 sq. ft. market in a renovated space in an historic district is part of a small chain of supermarkets. The client's request was that KDI adapt an existing decor package into a space that has ceiling heights that vary from 10 to 20 ft. in the open truss areas. Since the space is wide and shallow and the aisles short, every bit of space was premium. The new design emphasizes three "rooms" or "halls" that were determined by the different ceiling heights. By stressing color in the architectural elements and altering and relocating signage to suit the assorted ceiling heights, each space becomes an effective selling venue. The floors are unified by being finished in "antique russet," acid stained concrete with assorted accents. The perimeter drywall areas are painted vibrant red, gold and beige while the exposed trusses are finished in a "squash" color. Suspended maple trellis grids with track lighting are suspended from the ceiling. Light maple laminates are used for fixtures while "maze weave" laminates cover the cabinetry. Adding color throughout are the large wall murals, quotes about food, company slogans and digital murals. KDI delivered a creative package that met the client's goal. Says KDI, "the client's input and ideas allowed us to create a unique, cost effective store interior."

Above left: The surround of shelving for the wine/liquor area creates a warm setting for the café.
Left: Large murals—some digitally produced and others hand painted—add color and identification to produce.
Photography: PhotOregon.

This page: KDI combined large wall graphics and food quotes with logo embellished hanging banners printed on canvas textured vinyl. Together they "brand" and create an inviting ambiance for the market.

King Design International

Gelson's
Irvine, California

The design solution for the Gelson's Market in Irvine, CA called for a fun, over-the-top, sort of ambiance spiked with Italian historical references. The design as envisioned by KDI was for a Southern California style overlaid with Italian flair in the large sculptured architectural relief graphics, marbleized foam trims and the oversized chandeliers up-front in the checkout area. The upscale decor was underscored by the bold graphics that are used to affect the unique and individualized departments that fit into the niches around the market perimeter. Easily seen from across the store, these strong architectural features and graphics clearly define and identify the spaces. Trellises, overhead elements and specialty lighting in the service areas further enhance these shops-within-the-shop. The inspiration for the color and materials palette is Southern California: pastel blues, peaches and creams accented with natural wood tones. The floors are paved with ceramic tiles that emulate natural stone. Says the designer, "We are always excited with the fun challenges presented by this client to provide one-of-a-kind and over-the-top design and decor features."

Above: The specialty meat/cheese alcove. The back-lit panels in the cornice attract attention to this space.
Left: The clock tower stands in front of the floral shop which is distinguished by the post and trellis facade that carries the specialty lighting.
Photography: Long's Photography.

This page: *The signage is strong, bold and fun-filled with color and artwork. The specialty lighting enhances each area with its own one-of-a-kind look.*

King Design International

Supermercados Unicasa, C.A. ESP Margarita—EDO.NUEVA Venezuela

True to the "International" in its name, KDI made a foray into Venezuela to design this 22,000 sq. ft. market which is part of the Supermercados Unicasa chain. The design brief from the client was to create an upscale setting that would appeal to both the locals and tourists who vacation here. For this, KDI created a simple, straightforward layout with a power aisle that leads from the entrance through the separate islands, all encompassed in a contemporary envelope. The large structural columns were incorporated into the decor program and became visual focal features. The problems caused by the transitions in ceiling heights were overcome by the effective use of the decorative materials. Sign-age is minimal but the architectural elements—such as the colonnade around the seafood shop—highlight the various departments. A gracious, open feeling in the market is evidenced by the wider aisles and the mini-extravaganza at the meat boutique where shoppers are invited to sit on bar stools at the counter while ordering their cut-to-order meats. KDI's design has raised the standard for market design in this part of the world since this project has been widely reported on in the South American trade press. It is visible proof of what KDI says of its capabilities, "Our planning and engineering department has the capability to provide exceptional 'value engineering.' This is done without losing the initial design intent of the sign or décor element.

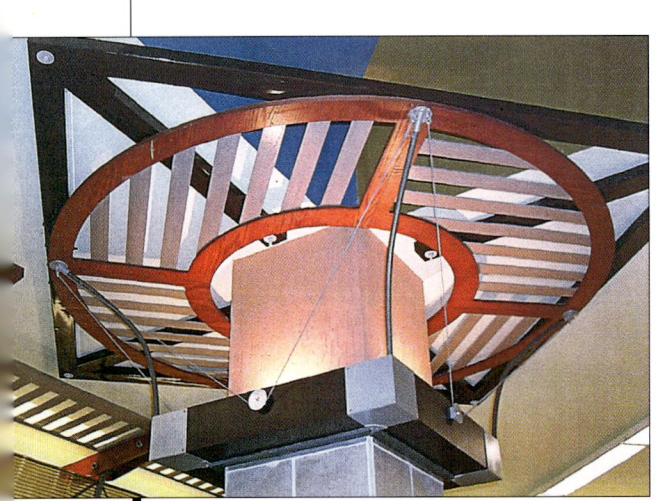

Above left: Colonnade enclosing the seafood shop.
Far left and left: Unique ceiling treatments add to the ambiance.
Photography: Supermercados Unicasa, C.A.

Lind Design International

130-17 23rd Avenue
College Point
New York 11356
800.297.5267
718.463.1100
718.463.0075 (Fax)
www.linddesign.com
www.supermarketdesign.net
ldplans@aol.com

Lind Design International

Quality Foods
Comox, BC, Canada

The award-winning supermarket (Canadian Independent Retailers' "Supermarket of the Year") was designed by Lind Design in response to the client's desire for "something different." Located in a new and developing suburban town near an air force base and populated with professionals and semiprofessionals, the design concept could be called "Northwest with a touch of New York." The freestanding, contemporary wood and stone 35,000 sq. ft. Quality Foods market ties in with the neighborhood, however, the interior is quite a departure from the nearby competitive, big-box stores. Though the spacious interior with its 30 ft. deck ceiling has two entrances, the main entry is into the floral and Produce areas while the other brings shoppers into the all-important, multi-fenestrated café. Since the produce department is separate from the rest of the fresh foods—it was imperative to the store's success that shoppers be drawn from one end of the market to the other and that trip across be a true shopping adventure. The answer was the "monumental" Kitchen Hearth that dominates the opposite

Above: *A view from the Cellar in the Sky on the second level. The unique cheese island is in the foreground.*
Right: *The grid over produce island caries highlighting spots.*

106

side of the market. It is a beacon that draws shoppers to the active rotisserie and the area where the assorted fresh foods and meals prepared to go are located. The wall of "brick" extends up from the floor to the ceiling and it serves to bring attention to the "Cellar in the Sky" department: a cookware/kitchenware/giftware boutique on the second level.

Above right: *A closer look at the cheese island with its bright yellow and white stylized awnings.*
Right: *The faux brick hearth of the kitchen area dominates the end of the market and brings attention to the shop above.*

Above left: The striped awnings that extend off the yellow panels carry the area signage.
Below: The individual "shops" are identified by big architectural elements such as the rich wood paneling in seafood market and the glistening copper hood and enclosure of the bakery.

The colors throughout are upscale and sophisticated—and comfortable—for this Northwest locale. Rich burgundy, deep purple, and dark green are played against the terra cotta color of the vinyl shale floor. In the produce area the vinyl floor is laid in a bold basket weave pattern of muted greens which contrasts with the burgundy cases sitting upon it. Suspended from the dropped ceiling are wood trellises dripping vines and foliage. At the opposite end of the store a rich, yellow/orange color is added that sparkles against the cool white walls. Accenting bands, moldings and cornices of a deep purple contrast with the walls and also accentuate the signs that appear as striped awnings angled off the diamond patterned yellow/orange panels.

To identify the various perimeter "shops," the designers created distinctive signage and settings above eye level. The glowing copper hood over the bakery and the unusual treatment of the surrounding area makes this a standout. The stainless steel cases of the seafood market are further enriched by the slick, gridded fascia of wood veneer and applied brass covered, cutout letters. To further promote the feeling of "shopping around" there are service-oriented island kiosks devoted to cheese and cake decorating. They are distinguished by the burgundy skeletal construction and the yellow and white striped awnings above. A staircase leads to the Cellar in the Sky where shoppers can find gourmet cookware and kitchenware as well as a large community meeting room. Cooking classes and seminars are conducted up here. For client and customer alike, this new design has proven effective. "It is a place to explore—to discover and to enjoy. There is a feeling of warmth as well as freshness and wholesomeness. As the client said, 'This store really works!'"

Right: Entrance to the "Cellar In The Sky" cookware/gift shop.
Center: A view of the gift shop.
Below: The faux brick wall treatment.

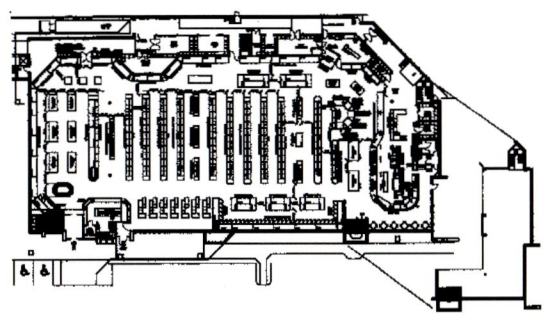

Lind Design International

Grande
Trujillo Alto, Puerto Rico

On this page: The Old San Juan architectural flavor is captured in the colorful produce area.

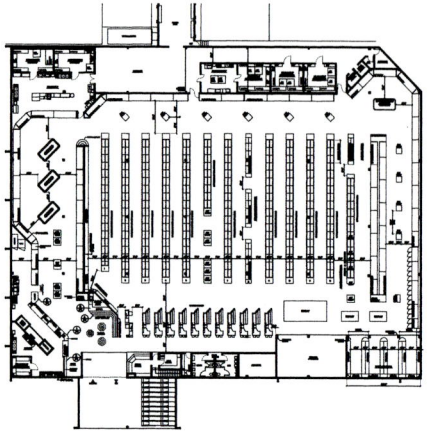

To design an upscale, sophisticated and fun supermarket for the residents of Puerto Rico requires going to the source for inspiration. The client wanted "a different look and a different way of showing products" than is usual in other Puerto Rican supermarkets. Working with Gary Lind of Lind Design, what evolved for this 40,000 sq. ft. Grande is a mercado: an outdoor marketplace concept. To get the feeling and create the desired ambiance, the designer took the colors, textures, architectural details—and the "flavor" of Old San Juan as the inspiration and researched that area thoroughly. Even the lamp posts and the bracketed street lamps that add to the out-of-doors feeling are authentic, the same as those standing in old San Juan. Terra cotta colored vinyl shale flooring was used to further the outdoor market place atmosphere. For this market Lind Design also came up with a new concept in decor. Instead of constructing costly curtain walls and permanent soffits, the designers created a series of architectural elements and decorative signage that can be suspended from the 22 ft. open deck ceiling. This is not only more economical but allows the client greater flexibility for the future: expanding or constricting areas, changing locations, etc.

Dropped trellises, arches, and decorative cornices carrying the departmental signage can be seen throughout the mercado. A 12 ft. street partition wall was constructed that divides the mercado from the central grocery sales area. Nowhere is the Old San Juan inspiration more apparent than in produce where the perimeter walls are treated like facades of the Spanish Colonial buildings. The authentic wall bracket lamps, the louvered shutters, the fan windows and everywhere the dripping flowers and foliage that fill and spill out from the San Juan balconies and sills, all help to create the desired setting. In this area the color palette is predominantly greens, yellows and white and the giant photomurals that serve as the backgrounds for the signage are framed in green. These colors are complemented by the rich blue of the cases and the terra cotta flooring. In the meat department the colors consist of deeper reds, orange, and teal blue accents. The Cava de Vinos (wine shop) stands out with its teal and vibrant red-violet facade and shoppers are invited to enter through an arcade trimmed with bracketed lamps, stylized turquoise awnings and more green foliage. In addition to an authentic Puerto Rican café, grande boasts of a rotisserie and bake shop as well as a flower shop at the entrance which is highlighted by the flower and awning bedecked, open peaked construction. The fact that the market works effectively and efficiently is further enhanced by the acceptance by the customers who enjoy shopping in a space filled with "local color." "The mercado is not only filled with attractively merchandised food products but it is brimming over with history, heritage and tradition."

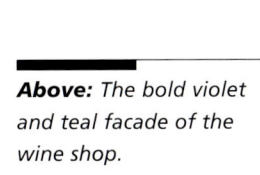

Above: The bold violet and teal facade of the wine shop.
Center & below: Some examples of the suspended architectural signage and decorative elements that are used in this design.

111

Lind Design International

Delchamps Primier
Mandeville, Louisiana

Above: A view of the partition that serves as the Tudor period wine shop on one side and the roadside farm stand on the other.

Below: The bases of the built-in cases in produce are covered with recycled wood to match the rustic woodwork on the soffit.

The Delchamps Primier store is based on the theme that the world is a village. The design team of Lind Design took bits and pieces from around the country—and beyond—to create the varied out-of-doors settings found in the 68,000 sq. ft. supermarket in Mandeville, LA. The market is located in a "high end" suburb of New Orleans and caters to a worldly clientele. The sleek contemporary building belies what is enclosed under the 28 ft. open deck ceiling. Because of its spaciousness, the designers took advantage of the height to create a second level for offices and for the café to extend up into. This market, which was selected as the "Store of the Month" by Progressive Grocer magazine, is dedicated to affecting "a creative, fun but focused shopping experience." A tour of the store moves the shopper in time, place and space from Tudor England (the wine shop) to a rustic, roadside farm stand of the 1930s (produce) to the retro graphics of the 1950s (deli and bakery) to a small fishing village's wharf and bait shack that is lost in time (seafood). With a full palette of colors, materials and textures, shoppers discover their way on this tour as the well-defined signs and suspended architectural elements lead the way.

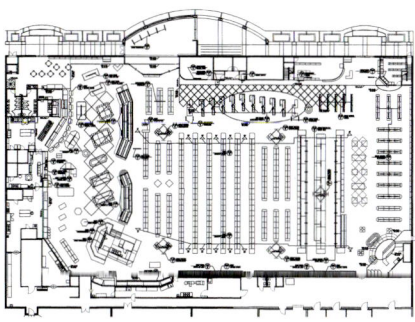

The three-story, brick hearth at the opposite end of the market serves as the focal draw to the deli area. A sweeping facade of awnings and gooseneck lamps is suspended out from the perimeter wall to encase and emphasize this area and the brick hearth which is the "heart of the design." The active rotisserie and other prepared food stations are clustered here. "This is a watershed store design where assorted new ideas and construction concepts all come together and combined with the novel three dimensional graphics make a distinctive statement for Delchamps Primier."

Above: The big, sweeping fascia over the deli area with the three-story brick hearth extending up to the ceiling.
Below left: The Tudor village wine shop

Below right: Sepia toned, photo blow-ups of historical local scenes add to the "local flavor" of the store.

113

Lind Design International

Price Chopper
Plattsburgh, New York

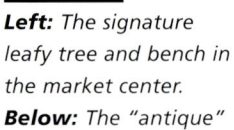

Situated in Plattsburgh, near the Canadian border, is the 68,000 sq. ft. Price Chopper supermarket. The designers were challenged to " create a warm and inviting fresh market center utilizing a design concept and materials palette that would be 'comfortable' for all demographics." The "comfort level" is what makes the "market center" so accessible and thus successful. Under a deep ocher ceiling and surrounded by warm, neutral beige walls with slip-resistant, terra cotta tiles on the floor, the center is highlighted by two Price Chopper signature elements: a floor-to-ceiling tree surrounded by a stone bench and an "antique" clock. The "tree" is built around a structural column and become a strong focal element in the design. The produce area is further enhanced by the weathered wood cartons and crates used to support some of the fruits and vegetables as well as the strong blue/green graphics-sign on the perimeter wall which is faced with squares of wood veneer.
Fluorescents are laid into the metal grid suspended over the produce area and spots are added for highlighting the product display.

Left: The signature leafy tree and bench in the market center.
Below: The "antique" clock and views of the produce department.

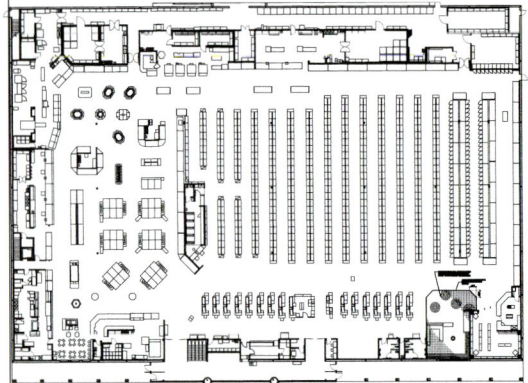

114

Each area or "shop" is highlighted by its own graphic surroundings and with architectural elements. The bakery is easily recognized by the wide curving copper-toned hood above and the wall of pseudo-brick ovens beneath it. The natural wood tables and display cases continue the arc of the hood and goose neck lamps and dimensional signs accentuate the hood's presence. FRP boards simulate ceramic tiles on the walls of the sushi and seafood areas. The black tiles and the black cases complement the Japanese-style roof suspended over the sushi shop while a wave-like, graphic design wraps around the soffit of the seafood area. Colorfully-illustrated, blackboards set above the blue tiled wall promote the daily fresh specials. The lattice work gazebo accented with flags, foliage and yellow and white striped awnings becomes a "shop-around experience" for lovers of imported cheese. Each "shop" has its own distinctive look and ambiance to create a spirited and fun feeling. The design that Lind Design created was focused on getting the most effect for the money and finding and utilizing materials that would stretch the client's budget. The success of the design and its adaptability have made it a great prototype for future Price Chopper markets.

Above: The open, Japanese-style roof is suspended over the Sushi shop
Center: The dimensional, wraparound graphics that define the seafood department
Below: The latticework cheese gazebo island on the floor.

Lind Design International

Guiliano's Fresh
Norfolk, Virginia

The 17,000 sq. ft. Guiliano's Fresh caters to upscaled shoppers. The design offered by Lind Design stresses the feeling of an outdoor village under the blue, 28 ft. open deck ceiling which is illuminated by metal halide uplights. Reinforcing the outdoors theme is the terra cotta stained concrete floors and the farmer's market ambiance of Produce where recycled woods are used to face the bases of the built-in wall cases and finish the soffit over the displayed vegetables and fruits. A French Provincial-inspired facade sets the mood for the Boulangerie (bakery) while a turn of the last century, red brick, shop front for Kansas City Stockyards, with red and white striped awnings, highlights the meats department. The designers captured the essence of a New England wharf for the seafood area and surrounded a centrally located hearth/tower with a trellis that could be enhanced with hanging salamis, cheeses and decoratives. This "hearth" is the source for rotisserie products, pizzas and the gourmet prepared dishes-to-go. Copper arches connect the grocery gondolas to affect an outdoors archway or arbor while hanging trellises and grips help to delineate special areas and support departmental signage. "The international feeling of Guiliano's has been underscored by unifying various main street facades into one complex, but visually satisfying, multi-ethnic village of fresh and wholesome food products."

Above: Produce area.
Left: The backery Boulangerie.

Left: The fresh fish wharf in blue, white and yellow with the 19th century Stockyards facade for meats beyond.
Below left: The hearth for the rotisserie/pizza and prepared foods island is surrounded with a trellis for hanging decorative elements.
Below right: Pointed metal arches connect the grocery gondolas for an arcade effect.

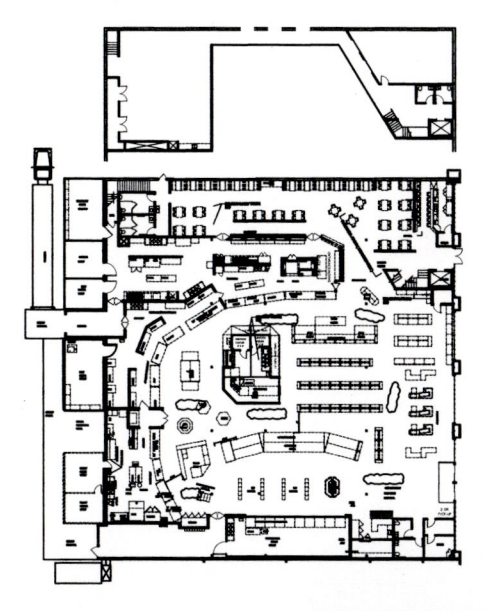

Right: The restaurant is tucked away under the balcony. The building facades continue around to become the setting for wines.

117

Lind Design International

Gourmet Garage
Scarsdale, New York

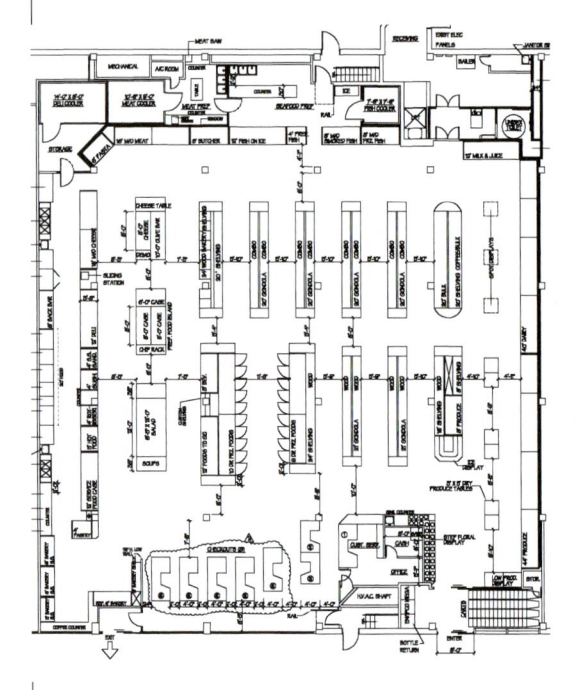

Above and below: The produce area is dominated by the graphic signage. Stainless steel and rough wood fixtures add texture to the setting.
Architect: Rosenbaum Associates, AIA.
Graphic Design: Grid 2.

118

Gourmet Garage started out in the Soho, section of New York City, as a whole new concept in affordable gourmet groceries presented in what was previously a garage. The enormous success of the store and its concept convinced the owner to go uptown—way uptown—into the affluent suburb of Scarsdale where the company's motto—"Shop like a chef" seems to resonate just as it does in Bohemian and artsy Soho. The new store has 11,500 sq. ft. of sales space and the store is strong on fresh perishables and prepared foods. Featured in Gourmet Garage are: produce, dairy, fresh service seafood and butcher shop, and salad, cheese and coffee bars. Lind Design not only planned the space to have a strong industrial/urban look but retained the existing concrete ceiling to enhance that look. The designers specified "industrial materials—real materials—natural materials" to create the desired ambiance. There are the stainless steel cases for the "high tech Soho look" surrounded by natural wood, concrete, diamond plate panels, and slate floors underfoot. Ceramic tiles appear on the walls and floors of the prep areas and white ceramic squares cover the columns which are banded with smaller, red tiles. The layout allows for spot merchandising; the designers accented the locations with a combination of metal halide, fluorescent and ED-17 spots—"to create a theatrical feeling in the store." Throughout there is a strong sense of color—primarily confined to the graphic facia that fills the perimeter walls. These powerful graphic "statements" "create the look and feel of being in Soho." Bold blocks of red, green and yellow, framed in stainless steel, band the walls and carry the "message"—"Shop like a Chef" as well as quotes from magazines, newspapers, chefs and food personalities. These copy blocks alternate with graphic images of the products being offered below. The Mondrian-inspired signs unify the market while also identifying the various specialty areas in it. Surrounding the signs are off-white walls and the coffered concrete ceiling is also light. One of the highlights of Gourmet Garage is the island display of olives, olive oils and assorted condiments. The stainless bins are filled with mouth-watering morsels and surrounded by imported and artisan cheeses and other party specialties. The Scarsdale grocery shoppers have already made Gourmet Garage a "must-stop, must-park" place to shop. The fun and free Soho spirit lives on and thrives in Scarsdale.

Top right: *The island display of Olives, oils and condiments.*
Right: *The Delicatessen is also the Fresh Service Butcher Shop where the meat is shown in stainless steel cases.*
Left: *A detail of the signage/graphic in the Dairy area.*

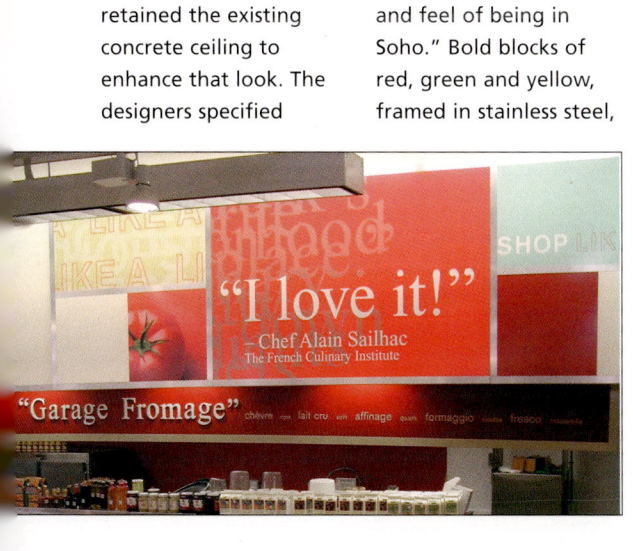

Lind Design International

PSK Foodtown
Brooklyn, New York

In an area of Brooklyn that is undergoing a renaissance with new retail stores, cafes and cultural centers blossoming, the owners of the 10,000 sq. ft. PSK Foodtown called upon Lind Design to renovate and redesign their market and make it more compatible with what is going on around it. The client's request was that the space with its 11'-6". ceiling have a "warm and homey feeling—like a family kitchen" rather than a market. Shoppers attracted by the new facade of terra cotta, green and beige ceramic tiles will find themselves surrounded by the same palette inside. Working with a palette of warm, earthy colors and natural wood, cornices, cabinets and floating ceiling elements, the result is a warm and welcoming space. The suspended, open fretwork cornices that front the Fresh-To-Go and other "shops" on the perimeter walls are further enhanced by the artwork that echoes the fretwork motif on the kitchen cabinets on the prep walls. These cabinets add to the kitchen look as do the ceramic tiles beneath. Throughout, the light woods provide the dominant material note while floors are finished in vinyl composition tiles in bold patterns of terra cotta and soft teal strongly accented with black and white. A giant floating wood shape, accented in black, hovers over the fruit and vegetable display and it carries the highlighting of this area.

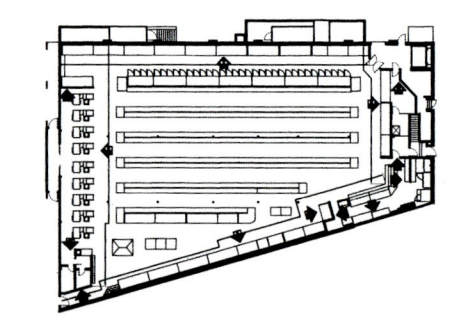

Above: Unique woodwork and floating ceiling panels define this store.

120

Marco Design Group

235 East Main Street
Suite 107
Northville
Michigan 48167
248.374.2360
248.374.2363 (Fax)
sales@marcodesigngroup.com
www.marcodesigngroup.com

Marco Design Group

Busch's
Farmington Hills, Michigan

"A world of difference—your food store" is Busch's new logo line and to interpret that "difference," Marco Design Group developed a new interior design concept, in conjunction with a store layout, to "achieve a highly integrated result with a consistent image at all levels." The levels the designers combined so effectively in this Farmington Hills 46,203 sq. ft. store are the architecture, the atmosphere, the merchandise presentation and—eventually—the total shopping experience.

The experience begins outside where the hand painted canopies extending out from the brick facade serve as the "welcoming mat" to the fun and feast-for-the-eyes that awaits within.

Above: Fruits and vegetables in brilliant color are hand painted on the curved, deep red awnings.
Right: Hand painted murals, painted ceilings and theatrical lighting featured in the produce section.
Photography: Laszlo Regos, Berkley, MI.

The interior concept makes effective use of bold architectural elements such as trellises and canopies to define service areas and heroic scaled tile floor patterns to "create a dynamic feel while visually anchoring the display fixtures." The store's layout is a "balanced shopping experience" with produce and flowers at the entry, meat and seafood at the rear and wine, deli and the bakery at the end of the trip. The perishable and service departments appear throughout the store's tour.

Above right: The exposed ceiling over the boldly-patterned aisles that help move the shoppers through the space.

Right: Canopies swoop over the seafood/meat service area. The back wall is covered with soft green, blue and creamtile in a wave-like design. The light blue floor adds a cool complementary touch.

Left: Jesters toast each other—and the shoppers—in the vast wine department.

Below: In the frozen area the fantasy figures are fashioned out of ice cream cones, scoops, sundaes etc. and finished in flavorful colors.

There is a "Shopper in Wonderland" feeling in this Busch's Market. The designers added a "cast of characters" who accompany the shoppers, point out the way, identify products and turn what might be a chore into a delight. The "Jester's Court" theme carries through with "Ladies-in-Waiting" as aisle markers, "Frozen Food Jesters" tossing scoops of ice cream over the frozen foods cases, "Whimsical Wine Jesters" toasting and coaxing shoppers into the wine department and the "King of Courtesy" presiding over the customer service desk. Lighting the decorative, thematic graphics are the recessed linear fluorescents in grocery, industrial high-bay metal halide lights over the aisles and flexible track lighting in produce, wine and bakery/deli.

124

The fun experience culminates at the check-out counters where internally-lit globes of whimsical design signal the shoppers to the open lanes. The light fixtures reaffirm Busch's "World of Difference" logo. For those with time and the desire to prolong their stay in these pleasant surroundings there is a Café with overstuffed seating set amid live trees and low magazine shelving. It is all part of the "stay with us a while and be entertained" atmosphere created by Marco Design Group.

Above: Near the entrance, under a trellis-arbor of greenery and twinkling lights is the flower department.
Below left: Graphic panels and illuminated globe fixtures mark off check-out.
Below right: The company's logo globe with the "World of Difference" message is located up front.

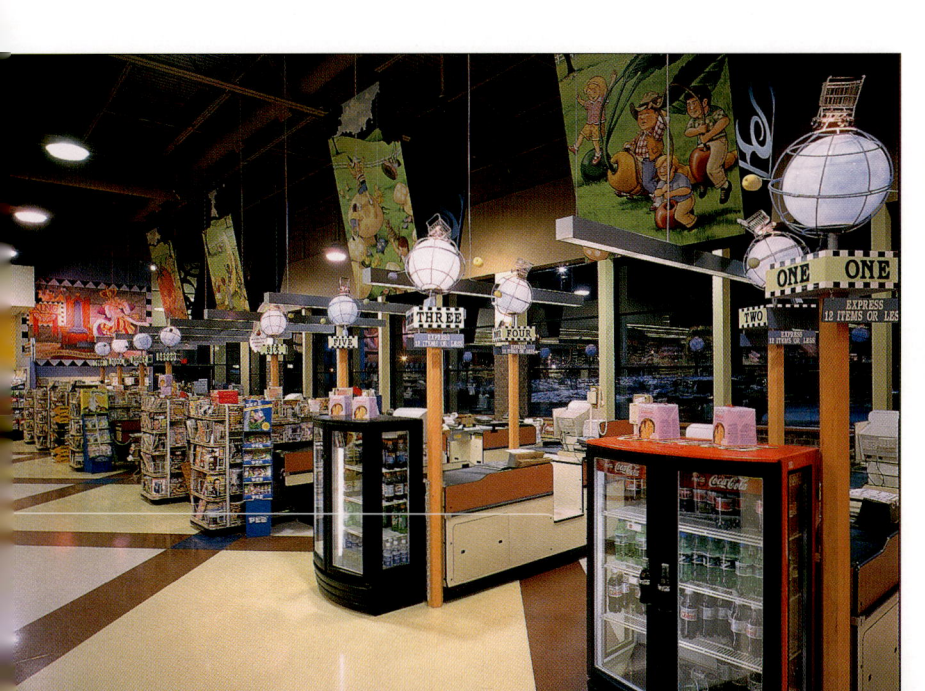

Marco Design Group

Sentry Foods — Hilldale
Madison, Wisconsin

This page: Murals of Wisconsin's farming community sets the stage for produce. An oversized, translucent star icon highlights the America's Market. The City Deli is recognized by its distinctive logo. An arched wood canopy over the aisle announces Great Harvest Breads.
Opposite: The seafood area glows with the blue neon light from the wave motif around the soffit. Metal fish sculptures varying from four to six ft. swim in a ceiling of translucent panels. Computerized lighting creates the watery illusion.
Photography: Laszlo Regos, Berkley, MI

The challenge to Marco Design Group was to expand and remodel this 54,000 sq. ft. market with a diverse customer base. While maintaining "an urban market atmosphere," "the environment language had to convey a comfort level to the upscale professional, to the frugal senior client, to the medical staff of the nearby hospital complex, and to the university student of the neighboring U. of W. campus." To this end the designers took a theatrical approach to the color and lighting used as well as the merchandise presentation to create "a very energetic shopping experience." Adding to the sense of drama and excitement are the varied floor patterns that add color and a sense of direction through the store. Some departments have been highlighted by the use of "upgraded" materials as in America's Market and the deli/bakery areas where granite composite tile was used. In the wine shop the floor is laid with wood. Lighting was used to further heighten the experience In produce the lighting is solely on the merchandise "to create a dramatic, theatrical atmosphere" and there is no ambient lighting. Adding to this is the "comfort balance" of exposed ceiling structure to floating ceiling fixturing. The ocean blue neon lighting and signage in seafood emphasizes the location and suggests freshness of product. Lights hang from an exposed wood grid ceiling in the wine department to create "a playful vineyard" effect while actually illuminating the stock. In the new layout produce, deli and bakery are on the left upon entering from the mall common area and America's Market—a prepared foods deli featuring "meals to go"—is on the right. Meats is on the back perimeter and seafoods connects perishables with groceries. Custom and standard fixtures and display cases are combined with homey kitchen cabinetry along the store's perimeter.

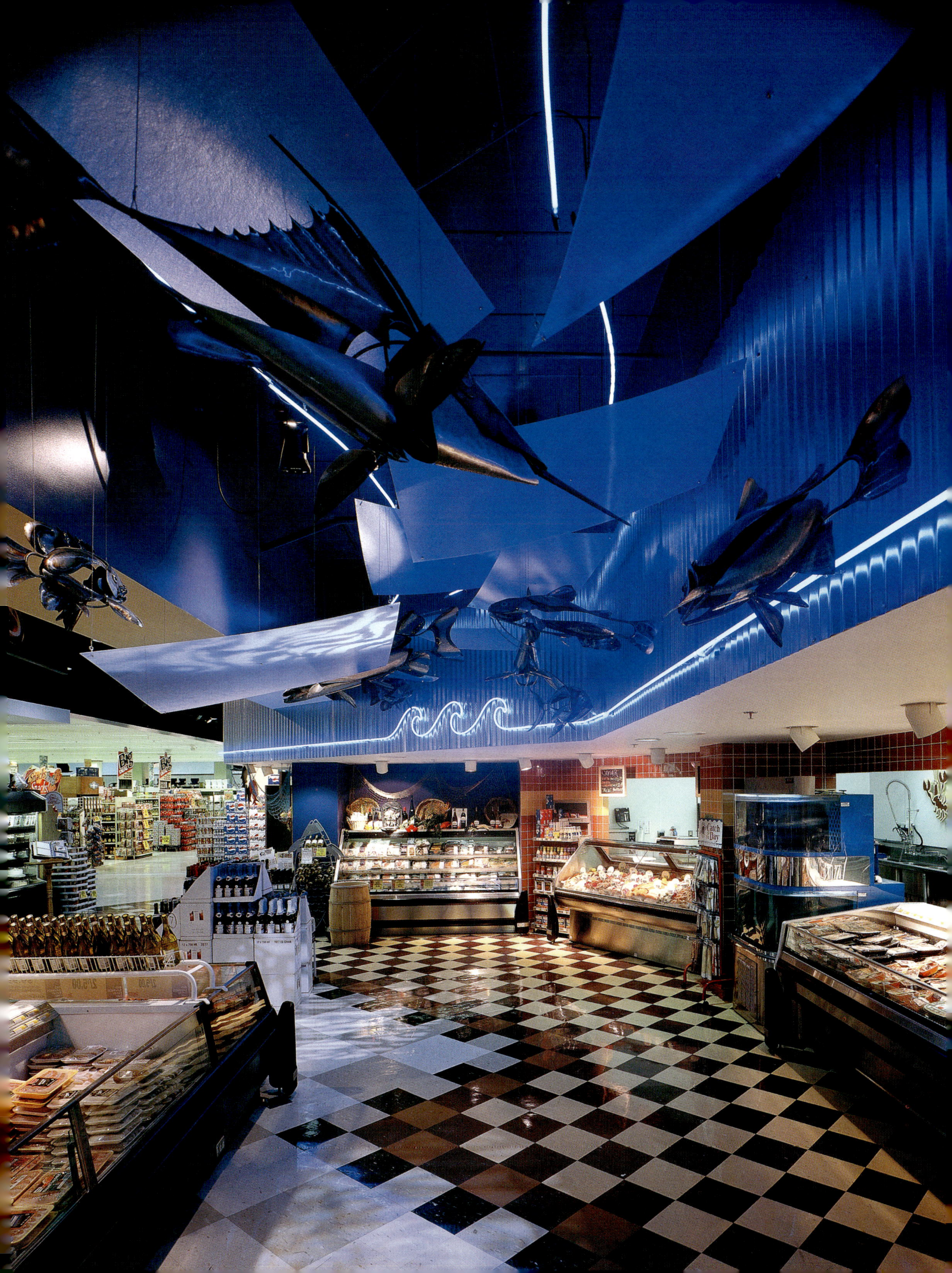

Marco Design Group

Bonson's Pick n' Save
Eagle River, Wisconsin

Right: Lower ceilings give the produce area a warmer and more finished look while the sophisticated lighting highlights the product and creates an upscale ambiance. The seven ft. high produce display contrast with the surrounding lower aisle displays making the customer feel they are surrounded by the fresh produce.
Below: The arts & crafts styling appears on the column tops and the signage located over the perimeter shops.

The 65,000 sq. ft. Bonson's Pick n' Save is located in Eagle River in northern Wisconsin. The market caters to tourists and the residents who have summer homes here. The objective was to create "a warm and comfortable" feel." Flexibility is key to the layout. The flexible merchandising allows departments to update and change. For example, the bakery affords numerous merchandising venues "that maintain the consumers' interest for repeat shopping." The easel-style, changeable message boards appear in many areas—easy to read/change—and thus flexible. Various display stations add to the flexibility/creativity in the visual merchandising and "they reinforce the concept of 'freshness' and 'something new.'" For the decor, the designers selected a fanciful interpretation of the arts & crafts style of almost a century ago. The signage reinforces the merchant's mission statement by reflecting a handmade, craft-like quality that gives this store a "point of differentiation from its competitors." The same design concept is used for the unique floor patterns and treatments, the textured wall coverings and the understated canopies. In the café, the arts & crafts style reappears in the stained glass ceiling and the art-deco mural.

Right: Changing floor patterns add interest to the movement through the market. Awnings, as in the cheese area, further the distinctive look.
Below: Patterned ceramic tiles appear on the back walls of the perimeter shops The "chalk-drawn" artwork in wood frames on the soffit above, carry through the arts & crafts style.
Photography: Laszlo Regos, Berkley, MI.

Marco Design Group   **Busch's Marketplace**
                           Livonia, Michigan

Above: Boldly-blocked floors and tiled columns provide the eclectic look in produce
Right: In the deli the diamond tile pattern of the back wall is played against the intricate pattern of the mosaic floor tiles. This leads to the wine area.
Photography: Laszlo Regos, Berkley, MI.

The Busch's Marketplace, a 43,000 sq.ft. supermarket in a new strip center in Livonia, MI was designed to be "upscale, yet affordable" and to offer quality products appealing to both the weekly shopper and/or the quick-stop shopper looking for a full meal, fresh produce, or a café. "An urban eclectic approach with a sophisticated attitude" was used in the design and decor to achieve an integrated result with a consistent look to the architecture, ambiance, and merchandise presentation. The citified marketplace atmosphere is achieved in produce through the use of custom mosaic tiles, specialty light sconces on the columns and hand painted wall murals. Josephine's Kitchen, the store's signature deli, picks up on the same theme with the brilliant awnings and the dimensional photomural departmental signs. Sweeping tile patterns and color balanced architectural valances add to the "richness" of the wine shop which transitions into prepared foods "thus allowing the consumer who is on-the-go to experience more fully the experience of the urban eclectic marketplace."

Right: In the café, sculptural decorative framing and hand painted street market banners "create a sense of fun."

Below right and left: The perimeter area has an exposed, neutral ceiling and mosaic tiles outline the seafood, deli and bakery—all "leading the customers naturally through the store." Note light sconces on the columns and undercounter lighting illuminating the walking tour.

Marco Design Group

Sentry Foods
Walworth, Wisconsin

To create the desired look and identity for the 56,101 sq. ft. Sentry Foods market in Walworth, WI, Marco Design Group returned to the earth and celebrated the workers of America's dairyland with graphic images and murals of the toilers and the dairy processing. The overscaled imagery explores the artistic style of the industrial era. Americana is the theme and the appeal is "to provide an entertaining food retail environment." To provide "a high level of comfort and pride for the value conscious community" and create a sense of nostalgia and welcome for the upscale tourists who shop here, the designers promoted Sentry Food's traditional brand images with a very effective departmental identity program. This put special emphasis on such in-store landmarks as America's Market, City

Above: The cheese area with Crestwood Bakery beyond. In the bakery "the playful icon signage" interacts with the striped awning to attract attention.
Right: A lowered ceiling and wood finishes plus an inviting floor design make the wine shop a definite destination.
Photography: Laszlo Regos, Berkley, MI.

Deli and Crestwood Bakery. Exposed ceiling structures at the perimeter support the feeling of a fresh food marketplace and also create a sense of theater and drama in produce. In contrast, the floating acoustical ceiling over groceries emphasizes value while facilitating the mechanical and lighting requirements for the area. Changing geometric patterns on the floor varying from the Mondrian-like rectangular arrangements of color in produce to a stylized plaid in flowers to a bold, chevron motif in cheese and Crestwood Bakery to the specialty wood finishes and the restrained zig-zag pattern in the wine shop, all add interest and delineate areas. All are executed in a full palette of muted and complementary neutrals and earth tones and further complemented by the brighter colors that flaunt the Americana-style awnings that distinguish the bakery and flower shop. A dramatic, decorative arch with an unusual hand painted mural and graphic embellishment is used to integrate fixturing and merchandising in meats. Throughout, the designers created strong visual focal points through the use of accent colors, graphics and theatrical lighting that makes a tour of this Sentry Foods a shopping pleasure.

Above: "We deliver on our promises" on overhead arches reinforces store philosophy.
Above right: The largest flower department in Sentry Foods gets full exposure with the attention-getting awning that delineates the open space.
Right: Produce benefits from the light focusing on the product display with no ambient lighting "to create a dramatic and theatrical atmosphere."

Marco Design Group

Sendik's Food Market
Brookfield, Wisconsin

"The Balistreri family wanted to have a big new store without losing the family neighborhood feeling and reputation. Our biggest challenge was to make sure the environment did not feel uncomfortable and cavernous—yet was warm and inviting." With this objective in mind, Marco Design Group approached the total design of the new 53,000 sq. ft. space. The approach was to clearly define and segment departments and create little stores within the larger store and incorporate a "sense of discovery and surprise" by strategically placing departments with high profiles so that the customer is not exposed to the whole store at once but shop in visual segments and find what he/she is looking for around the next curve of the aisle. To keep the store from appearing "cavernous," the ceiling planes were lowered to 11 ft. over the perimeter and service areas and raised to 14 ft. in groceries. In wine and produce the structural ceilings were left exposed. The new store, which is 2.5 times larger than the original, boasts a brick facade and is two stories high. The "U" shaped perimeter shell around the store allows for common prep and storage areas for ease in restocking. The market is on street level and there is a mezzanine with an exposed catwalk serving as an office. "It visually reinforces the approachability and service commitment of the retailer."

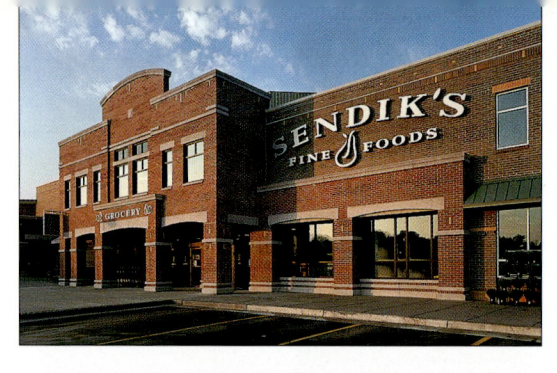

Top: The brick facade of the 53,000 sq. ft. Sendik's Fine Foods market.
Above and opposite: The floral & gift basket department featuring polished, stained concrete and rose trimmed floors, coolers and custom rose wood tables.
Left: Produce is enriched by the many photographic murals on the soffit over the product display.
Photography: Laszlo Regos, Berkley, MI.

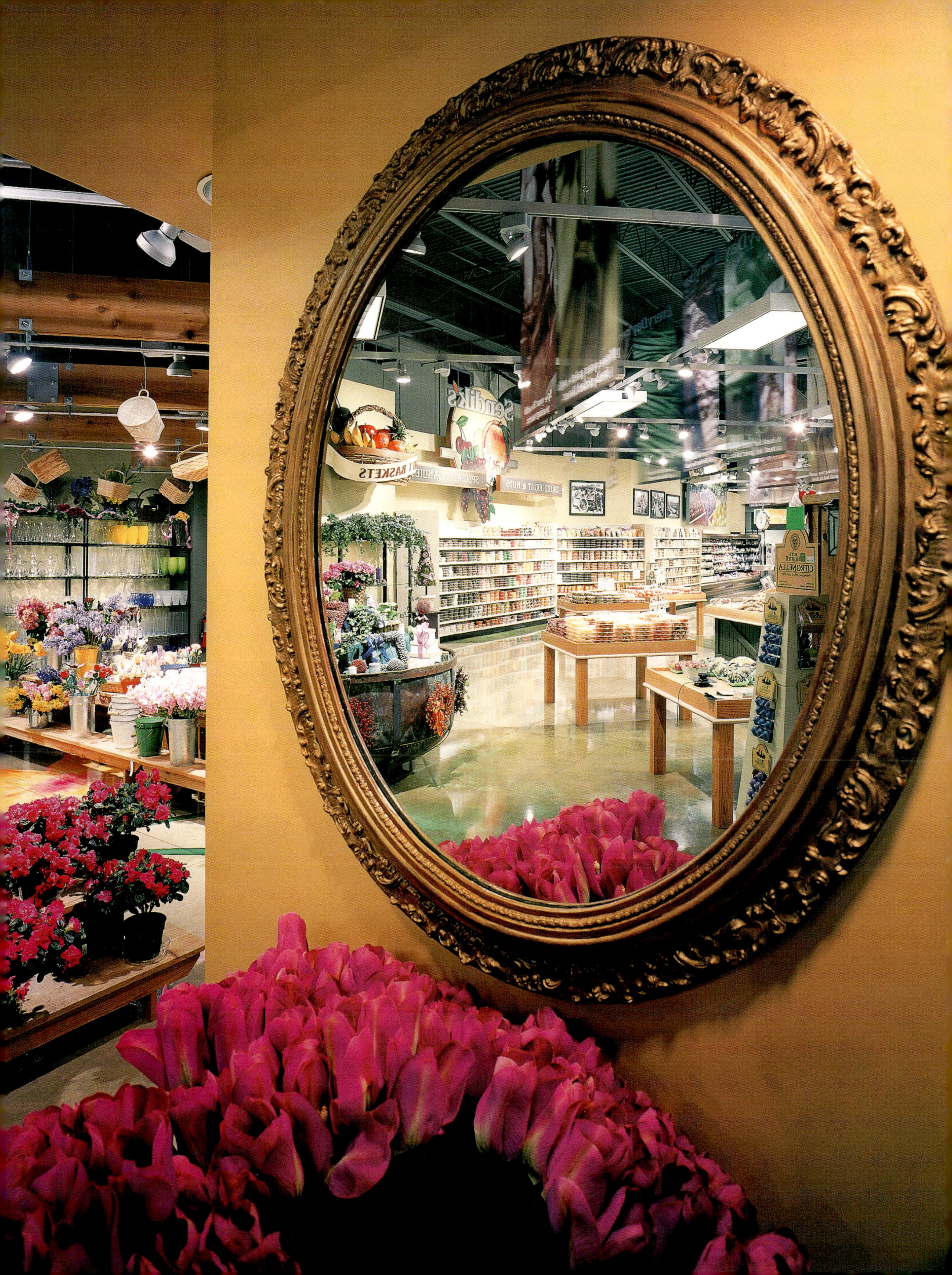

Left: The wine shop is a shop-within-the-shop and shows the merchant's commitment to selection, quality and volume.
Below left: In the bakery area the stained concrete floors and neutral colors tie in with the earthy gold tone of the soffit. Recessed fluorescents light up the space.
Below right: The coffee/tea boutique with amusing and colorful, semi-translucent hanging lamp shades and vintage label blow-ups.

A walk-in cooler makes the cheese area a must-see, must-visit part of Sendik's. The department is stocked with selections of both domestic and imported cheeses. Adding visual interest to the produce area set out under the exposed ceiling—in addition to the photomurals—there are semi-transparent scrims depicting the retailer's family members (the Balistreri's) going about their daily activities at the produce depot. This reflects on how fresh the produce is and on the honesty of the retailer. In the wine department—shop set off from the rest of the market—also under the exposed structural ceiling, the bottles are set out on rosewood shelves along the perimeter walls. An antique copper wine vat, now turned verde gris and weathered, serves as a central and focal display unit. Photo blow-ups of vintage wine bottle labels decorate the darkened walls over the shelves. For Marco Design Group, the credo for this project and in many of their other designs is "the approach to totally integrated design with architecture, lighting, layout, fixturing, merchandising and signage—working in concert—to achieve one continuous message." In Sendik's Fine Foods the message is "great value, best quality and unequalized family values."

Nebe International

2310 Fordham Street
Lubbock
Texas 79415
806.763.1984
806.763.1987 (Fax)
www.nebeinternational.com
norbert.nebeinternational.com

Nebe International

Save Mart Supermarket
Clovis, California

Right: The old train station theme is evident on the market's facade.
Below: The produce area is dominated by the long, wraparound mural of trains and fields of produce.
Photography: JQT Photographics

The 54,000 sq. ft. Save Mart Supermarket that opened in Clovis, CA reflects the community-minded thinking that is part of this chain's credo. Taking its design cues and inspiration from the location—an old train station—the design team of Nebe International created this neighborhood-friendly market. "It is always fun to have a specific theme, as in this case—the memories of an old train station," says Norbert Nebe, CEO of the design firm Nebe International.

Starting with the vertically-paneled facade with its peaked roof and an arcade running in front, the vintage train/railroad station theme takes over and the designers carried that theme into the interior with its open deck ceiling 16-18 ft. off the Armstrong covered floor. The 138 ft. long mural that is 6 1/2 ft. high—"probably one of the longest in the USA"—spreads out on the fascia over the wall stacked with fruits and vegetables in the fresh produce area. The trains, on the mural, seem to be zooming through the rows of verdant produce, drawn in forced perspective, while the sky above is filled with radiating bands of blue and yellow. A pair of old fashioned, black locomotives charge out off the wall that is loaded with fresh farm products. The produce is also displayed on tables set out under the fluorescent fixtures that streak across the space suspended down from the light colored ceiling.

The "antique" California produce logo designs are interspersed on the long mural that dominates this department. The deli & pizza area—one of the shops-within-the-shop—is distinguished by the corrugated metal awnings that project out over the foods on display in the open cases below. The shutters are painted with high gloss automotive paints and the artwork of the signage includes railroad signal flags. The prep area behind the aforementioned cases suggests a homey kitchen with cabinets above a bold checkerboard pattern of tile on the walls.

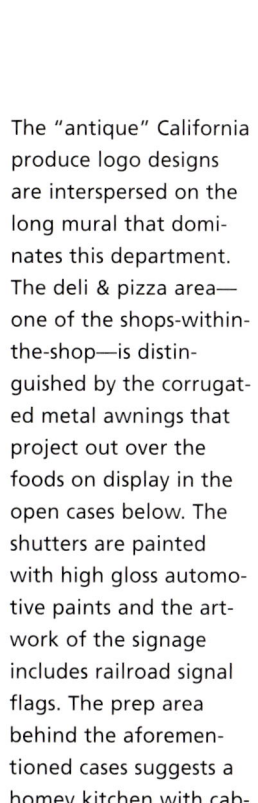

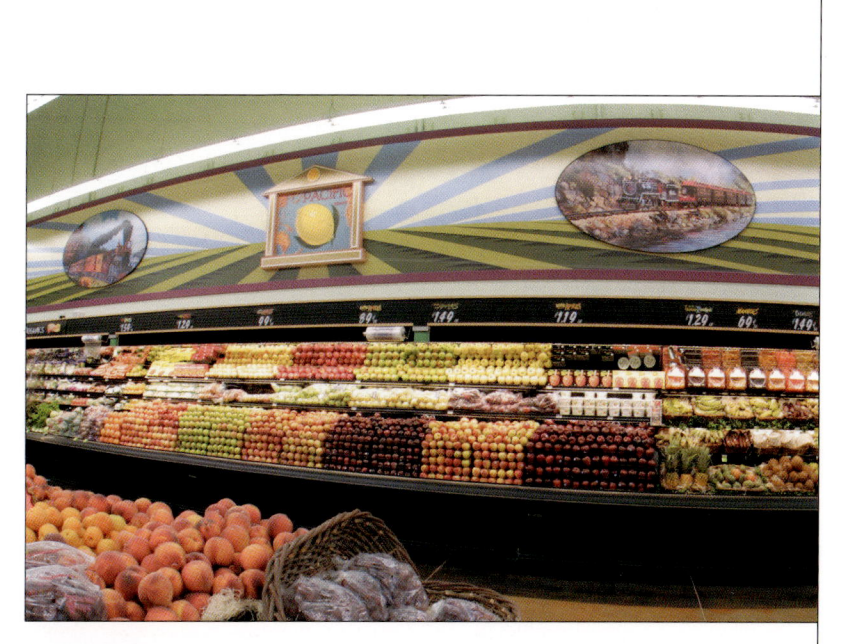

Above: The deli & pizza shop is highlighted by the high-gloss, metal corrugated awning and the graphic/sign with signal flags.

139

The train/railroad motifs abound throughout the market and the cleverly conceived markers—based on railroad graphics—show shoppers which foods are available at which "track." The designers have "precision routed" shoppers through the space by means of these assorted "arrival boards" that are furnished with interchangeable inserts. The black, white and red directional markers are readily picked out from the colorful atmospheric graphics that are used in the market.

Above & below: "Antique" graphics and photos of Clovis City add color, charm and a sense of period to the market interior.

Just as in the produce area, trains are chugging through dairyland. The mural here, a large format digital "wallpaper" with three dimensional lettering was created by Nebe International to keep the theme moving over the top of the refrigerated cases filled with milk, juices and such. Railroad style signage, in frozen foods explains where which products can be found. Photos of the city of Clovis—as it appeared 100 years ago—are used to create a collage over the refrigerated cases. Included in the montage of images is the old train station that once reigned where this market now stands. "The largest glacier" in California, according to the designers, appears here in the form of a giant wall mural with applied dimensional letters. Meat graphics and old fashioned pictures of vintage trains moving through the California landscapes sets the mood for the meat area. The motifs extend to the eight checkout counters where the red, black and white illuminated markers identify the lanes—or tracks. They remain in character with the "retro graphics" of "ancient" trains that appear on a nearby perimeter wall. For Norbert Nebe and his design team it was "rewarding to see how elements of railroad traffic could be incorporated into a retail food interior and still support the purpose of supermarket design: create an exciting place to shop."

This page: *Railroad markers, signboards and graphic elements appear throughout to keep shoppers "on track" while shopping and checking out.*

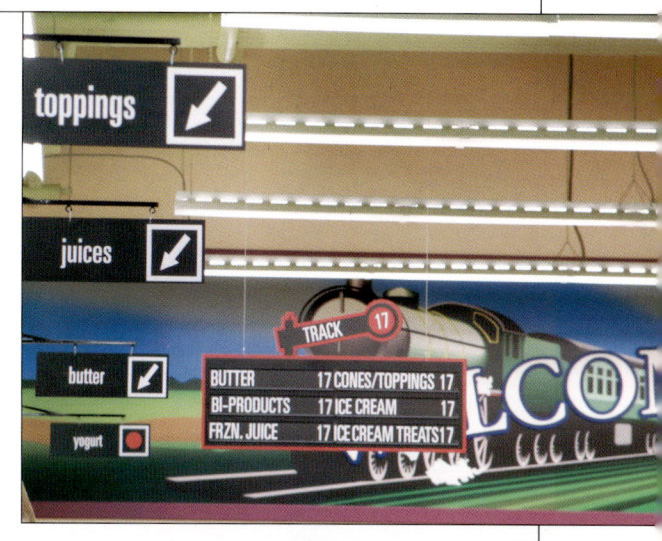

Nebe International

Vista Mercado
El Paso, Texas

Vista Mercado is a small, regional chain and the design for this 32,000 sq. ft. market, designed by Nebe International, blends with its location. It also becomes a relaxed and comfortable shopping oasis for the bilingual shoppers of this store located in the eastern part of El Paso in Texas. From its Mission-style, Spanish Colonial adobe facade to its soft, creamy coloring that ties in with the desert and the Mexican neighborhood, the market has a traditional feeling and is part of the local community. The management requested "a Spanish/Mexican marketplace"—and that is what they got!

Above: *The Vista Mercado sign on the Spanish Colonial, Mission-style facade introduces the gay coloration of the marketplace.*
Right: *The produce plaza, all sunny yellow, features hand-painted windows filled with produce and architectural trims.*
Photography: *JQT Photographics*

Right: *A terra cotta band of roof tiles, over the meat counter, highlights this shop with its ocher gold cornice design.*

There are two entrances into the interior with its open deck ceiling 18 ft. off the concrete floor which has been painted "desert tan" and then sealed. The assorted sheet rock and partially stuccoed walls are happy and harmonious pastel colors that clue the shopper into what is where in this "outdoors marketplace." Yellows, pinks, greens and terra cotta reds predominate and all of these colors are introduced in the signage on the facade under the rising sun logo. Architectural elements—reminiscent of the Mission-style architecture of two or more centuries ago—appear as arched frames over applied "windows" or dramatic, classic cornices over specialty shops within the market.

To create the look for the interior the design team created hand painted murals that depict Spanish-Mexican foods as well as a very distinctive "brush stroke" type of lettering that continues the hand crafted look of the space. Arched "windows" filled with images of fruits and vegetable are set into the sunny yellow stucco walls of the produce area. The walls are trimmed with terra-cotta colored moldings that suggest the out-of-doors facades of buildings facing a marketplace. The Spanish signs are emphasized while the English is used as subtitles for the mainly Spanish speaking clientele. The sun ray motif that appeared on the facade signage reappears behind the painted fruits and vegetables to create a sense of design continuity. The meat counter is also a shop-within-the-shop and a stylized, dimensional terra-cotta "roof tile" border underlines the distinctive signage and the artwork of assorted cuts of meat and sun rays in the arched windows under the ocher yellow crown molding. This area is painted yellow as well.

143

Left and below: The panaderia, the pasteleria and the pizzeria share the soft pink wall color accented with terra cotta. Arches over the artwork and straight crown moldings add to the exterior building look.

The market interior features individual "shops" that are detailed with architectural elements that enhance the concept of Mission-style buildings, in rich, pastel colors, surrounding an outdoor market in a make-believe town somewhere in Mexico. The open deck ceiling is painted out to further emphasize the outdoors experience and halide lamps are used for general lighting. The halide spots pick out and play up the graphics and wall signage. Adding to the desired Mexican ambiance is the Mexican Pizza shop, the bakery featuring Mexican specialties and the tortilleria. The designers also created front end shops for special vendors: ceramics, electronics, books and magazines. As the shopper travels through these easily accessible spaces, he or she finds themselves in soft, ice cream tinted environments that vary from sunny yellow to pale pink in the panaderia (bakery) and to the pasteleria where shoppers will find all sorts of desserts and treats. Attached to the pasteleria—under a floating canopy topped with a rich, reddish terra cotta crown molding—is the pizzeria with pre-prepared as well as build-your-own services. The same pale, dusty pink appears on the textured wall over the dairy cabinets where the terra cotta moldings also appear over the painted graphic appliques. A pistachio colored wall highlighted with an overscaled dentil molding of emerald green identifies the many enclosed refrigerated wall cabinets filled with helados (ice cream) a very popular Mexican treat. Suspended throughout the market are signboards that serve as directionals. The Vista Mercado logo fills in the central semicircle while the balance of the sign combines the accent trim colors: emerald green, golden ocher, black and the red terra-cotta color. Adding to the fiesta-like atmosphere are the colorful pinatas floating down from the dark ceiling. Norbert Nebe said, "We wanted our customers to enter the store and shout 'Viva!.' We intended for the Spanish customers to feel right at home and for the non-Spanish customers to enjoy some kind of Disneyland experience at a local level."

Above left: The helados area is soft green accented with emerald green. Dairy is pale pink.

Below: Directional sign featuring the Vista Mercado logo and the sharp accent colors used on the interior walls.

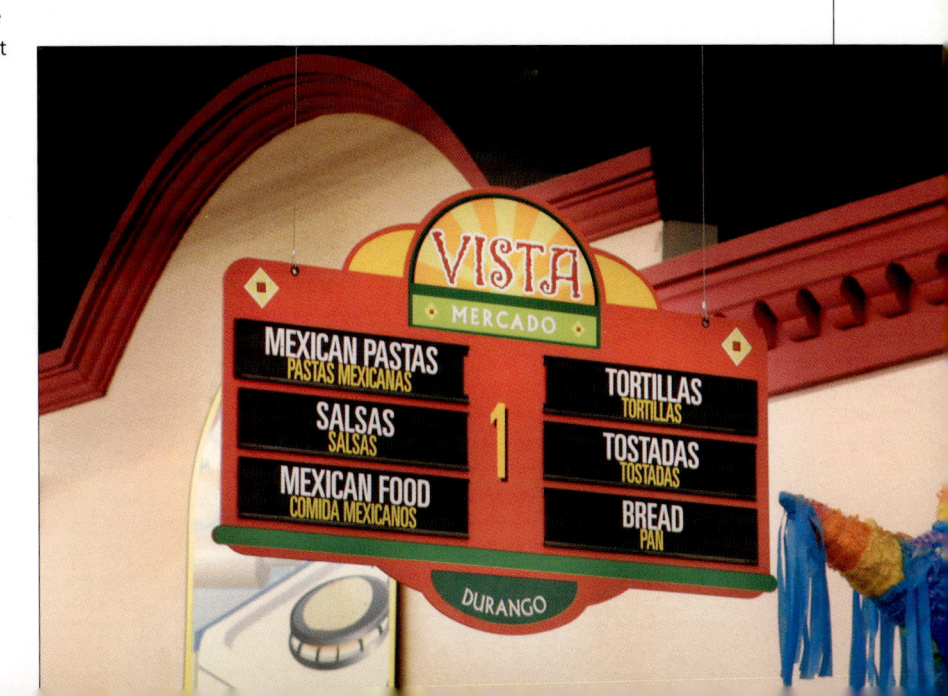

Nebe International

**Food Maxx
San Leandro, California**

Right: *The Food Maxx signage in yellow and blue sets the color theme for the interior.*
Below: *Fresh produce features warehouse-type displayers and double XX promotional signage.*
Photography:
JQT Photographics

The design directive couldn't have been more simple—or more emphatic: "create a fun environment in a price impact store." Knowing what was expected was only part of it, the problem was how to do it in this "budget minded" Food Maxx store in San Leandro, CA. The free standing, 65,000 sq. ft., stucco finished commercial structure is essentially a "no frills" building with partially cinderblock/partially sheet rock walls. How to do it? With color, more color and upbeat graphics!

Butter yellow and a rich warm blue color appear on the white facade of the market to introduce the signature colors and logo for Food Maxx. Nebe International, the designers, brought the same clear, primary colors inside the white shell and highlighted them with red. A blue molding strip marks off the perimeter walls at about 14 ft. and then allows the white walls to float up to the matching open deck, metal ceiling 20 ft. off the light, neutral gray linoleum covered floor. Forming a continuous accent band just under the blue cornice is a wavy pattern of yellow. The wall mounted departmental signage mimics the logo lettering and the red letters have blue "shadows." Adding to the whiteness and lightness of the space is the overall wash of halide light. Shoppers are led around the perimeter wall shops and thus introduced to the various freshness departments. "Massive signage, free hanging retail philosophy signs, directional signs, and up beat graphics" create the desired ambiance and also encourage the price aware shopper to venture fully throughout the space. The over 200 promotional and directional signs point up the price points, the promotions, the specials and the various shopping advantages in this market. The main aisle of the store features black category signs with red directional arrows indicating product location. Big price point reference signs on the end caps clearly highlight the specials. The eight checkout counters feature large white numerals on red circles which are part of the Double XX promotional signage found throughout the store.

"We wanted to create an environment through clean wall graphics and easy-to-read messages that signal a 'user friendly' warehouse store." "We wanted to make Food Maxx something very different from the usual 'no-frills dungeons' one usually associates with this type of market operation."

Above right: Fresh meat with 3D graphics and signage. The fresh bakery uses "quick turn" warehouse racks to suggest product freshness.
Right: The central grocery aisle with overhead directionals and price highlights on the end caps.

147

Nebe International **Blue Sage Supermarket
El Paso, Texas**

Above: *The logo/signage and colors that set the look for Blue Sage Supermarket.*
Below: *The produce area is all green while the meat department is blue and violet. Both areas are accented with "floating awnings" of desert sand.*

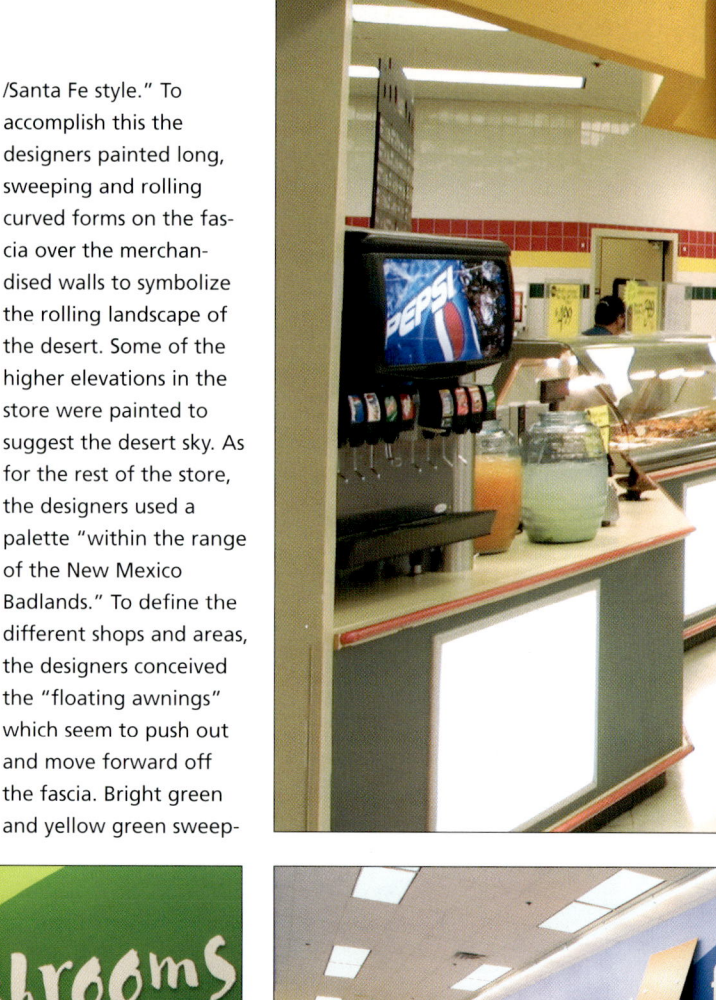

With expansive views of desert sunsets, is it any wonder that Nebe International used the colors of the Southwest to color the interior of this commercial, big-box building in El Paso, TX that now houses Blue Sage Supermarket; a new addition to a small chain of markets. Nebe also designed the logo graphics for Blue Sage and the subtle blend of blues, grays, greens, fuchsia and yellow carry over inside the 56,000 sq. ft. store with 22 ft. ceilings. The client's request was that the store reflect a "modern Southwest appeal" without crossing over into a typical "California/Santa Fe style." To accomplish this the designers painted long, sweeping and rolling curved forms on the fascia over the merchandised walls to symbolize the rolling landscape of the desert. Some of the higher elevations in the store were painted to suggest the desert sky. As for the rest of the store, the designers used a palette "within the range of the New Mexico Badlands." To define the different shops and areas, the designers conceived the "floating awnings" which seem to push out and move forward off the fascia. Bright green and yellow green sweeping shapes fill the fascia in the produce area while desert sand colored awnings break up the flat wall surface. Using a variety of fresh and fun typefaces, words-appropriate to the product display-become decorative elements as well as informational signs. Ocher golds, olive greens and beiges take over the patterning on the surrounding deli walls: the walls below are finished with similar colored ceramic tiles. Blues and violets take over to define the meat department. As in other areas, the designers specified sleek black counters and cases accented with red/violet stripes. The same, sharp fuchsia color appears over the seven checkout lanes. Adding an upscale sense of customer comfort are the wide aisles that also add to the spacious and open feeling of the market. Combined with the unique and sophisticated color palette, the clear and crisp lighting set into the dropped ceilings that border the perimeter shops and the clever graphic signage that is also decorative, Blue Sage comes across as something really different. "By using toned down Southwest colors and contemporary architectural shapes and three dimensional design elements, we hoped to 'move' this store beyond its four walls and create the incredible sensation of the desert spaces."

Above: The deli/bakery & salad area features the complementary, step-forward awnings.
Center: The checkout lanes are accented with bright red/violet numbers and the same rolling landscape lines featured on the fascia and the logo.
Below: A detail showing the Blue Sage color palette.
Photography: JQT Photographics

149

Nebe International

Super One Foods
Duluth, Minnesota

Left: The red, green and yellow 48 ft. tower that attracts highway riders to Super One Foods.
Below: The open, spacious deli area and the cafeteria-style restaurant beyond.
Photography: JQT Photographics

Driving up the highway to the "green fields" that surround the new Super One Foods market in Duluth MN, one can't help but be attracted to and intrigued by the massive, 48 ft. high landmark tower in red, green and yellow that stretches up before you. It heralds the arrival at the free standing, 70,000 sq. ft. store, part of a chain, that is highlighted by the backlit and channel-lit graphics and typography on the facade. There are two entrances into the 22 ft. high interior where Nebe International, the designers, created a design statement that suited the client's request—"Less is Better" and a look that is European in feeling: clean, open and spacious. Using "real food" photography, a full palette of soft and luscious pastel colors with striking accent colors added plus contemporary typography for signage, the result is a crisp and smart supermarket interior. Corrugated metal panels carry the mounted photo blowups and they serve as identifying medallions against the soft colored walls. Three dimensional letters are applied over the thematic copy that is painted on the walls. The fresh deli area is typical of the open and spacious feeling of the store. Adjacent to it is a very convenient and customer-friendly cafeteria where the deli and takeout foods can be "pretested" in the store. In the fresh produce area, a dropped ceiling around the perimeter wall carries the recessed lighting that illuminates the products offered on the wall hugging stands. The balance of the open deck ceiling, painted white, is filled with suspended halide light fixtures that provide the store's general lighting. The red, green and yellow logo colors, introduced on the tower outside, are used extensively for the wall signage: red and green for the cutout letters and yellow for the painted "Enjoy" copy. "Enjoy" is the store's theme word and it is incorporated into the signage and graphics. The Armstrong linoleum floors are off-white and accented with colors appropriate to the area.

Above and below:
Two views of the fresh produce department: the red, green and yellow wall graphics and the dropped ceiling grids that support the product's accent lighting.

Above: Category identifiers are suspended off curved brackets above the frozen foods cabinets.
Center: A dropped grid over the bakery floor display enhances the area and the product.
Bottom: The seafood and fresh meat shops.

To contrast with the white walls, are soft yellow painted areas such as the soffit in the deli department and the wide band across the bakery with its checkerboard motif in ceramic tiles on the back wall. The same motif is repeated on the floor in front of the illuminated cases. As in other areas, the corrugated metal wall plaques carry the photo graphics and the decorative red striped line ties the graphics and the signage together. Natural wood fixtures on the selling floor carry the freshly baked products. A dropped ceiling grid, with spots, adds to the atmosphere of the department and the visual appeal of the baked goods. In the frozen foods area the wall cabinets are identified by the oval blade signs on curved arms. The row of recessed lights in front of the cases adds to the prestige of the area.

Designing this store was a special treat for Norbert Nebe and his staff. "We have designed huge superstores in Europe and it was gratifying to see a retailer who wanted this approach—for its looks—in the U.S. The client gave us 'carte blanche' to do the logo as well as the exterior and retail identity. The client was delighted with the results and we were happy to do what we did."

Watt IDG

172 John Street
Toronto
Ontario M5T 1X5
Canada
416.593.7254
416.593.7940 (Fax)
prodmell@wattintl.com
www.wattintl.com

Watt IDG

D'Agostino
54th Street & 10th Avenue
New York, New York

The challenge for Watt IDG was "to build a new store that continues the family heritage of D'Agostino while evolving the overall look and feel of a contemporary grocer." In a relatively small and irregular space of 11,000 sq. ft., with various size columns that do not fit a regular grid, the designers had to come up with a design solution.

Upon entering the space, the customer is greeted with a fresh City Market that combines prepared foods, fresh produce and meat. "The overall intent was to allow for regular quick shops that may just be for dinner that night while still accommodating a complete offering for once-a-week stock-up shopping." The space is punctuated with floating ceiling planes and a unique rotunda appears over the butcher shop. Some of the irregularly-spaced columns became feature or focal elements and others were incorporated into the departmental or grocery shelving. The floors were covered with VCT tiles in black, gray and white and vinyl wood strip flooring was used to accentuate certain zones. The service areas were finished up to eight ft.; above there the side walls and ceilings were painted out. In some areas there were exposed brick walls.

Above: Entrance to D'Agostino on the ground level of a new 12-story apartment building.
Right: The produce department dominates the City Market with a dropped ceiling plane over it.
Photography: Richard Johnson, Interior Images

Above and right:
Views of produce area with vinyl wood strip flooring and hanging metal halide lamps. A sophisticated black, white and gray color scheme is used throughout.

Above: One of the several self-serve food stations for quick meal take-out. Black laminate and stainless steel highlight each station.
Right: The sleek, contemporary and upscale attitude of the store is seen at the entrance where the smaller scale carts are provided.

According to the designers, "This project continues to build on the New York tradition of the D'Agostino family. From the ubiquitous 'D'Ag Bag' to specific references in movies and TV shows using Manhattan for their setting, D'Agostino is New York's grocer. The grocery store is usually the anchor of the neighborhood, so we wanted a feeling of permanence and timelessness in order to maintain that position over time." In order to fit all the required elements into the allotted space, "Using the latest technology in refrigerated cases and systems control allowed us to put more into this store while inspiring some of the unique finishes selected." Throughout, the space was designed using a very upscale and sophisticated neutral palette of black, gray and white with silvery metallic laminates and striping. The company's signature red and green colors were used as accents on the signage. "Signage has been incorporated to build brand continuity, provide information of the unique offerings, and act as informational and directional communications for the customer."

The challenge was to design a store that would appeal to the new residential base developing in this neighborhood and not alienate any long-standing customers. "While shopping habits continue to evolve we wanted to build-in a level of flexibility that would allow for future opportunities and possible expansion to be explored. The overall integration of an operating strategy, a contemporary store design and strong graphic communications creates a compelling brand experience that is part of our mandate since starting our work with D'Agostino in 1980."

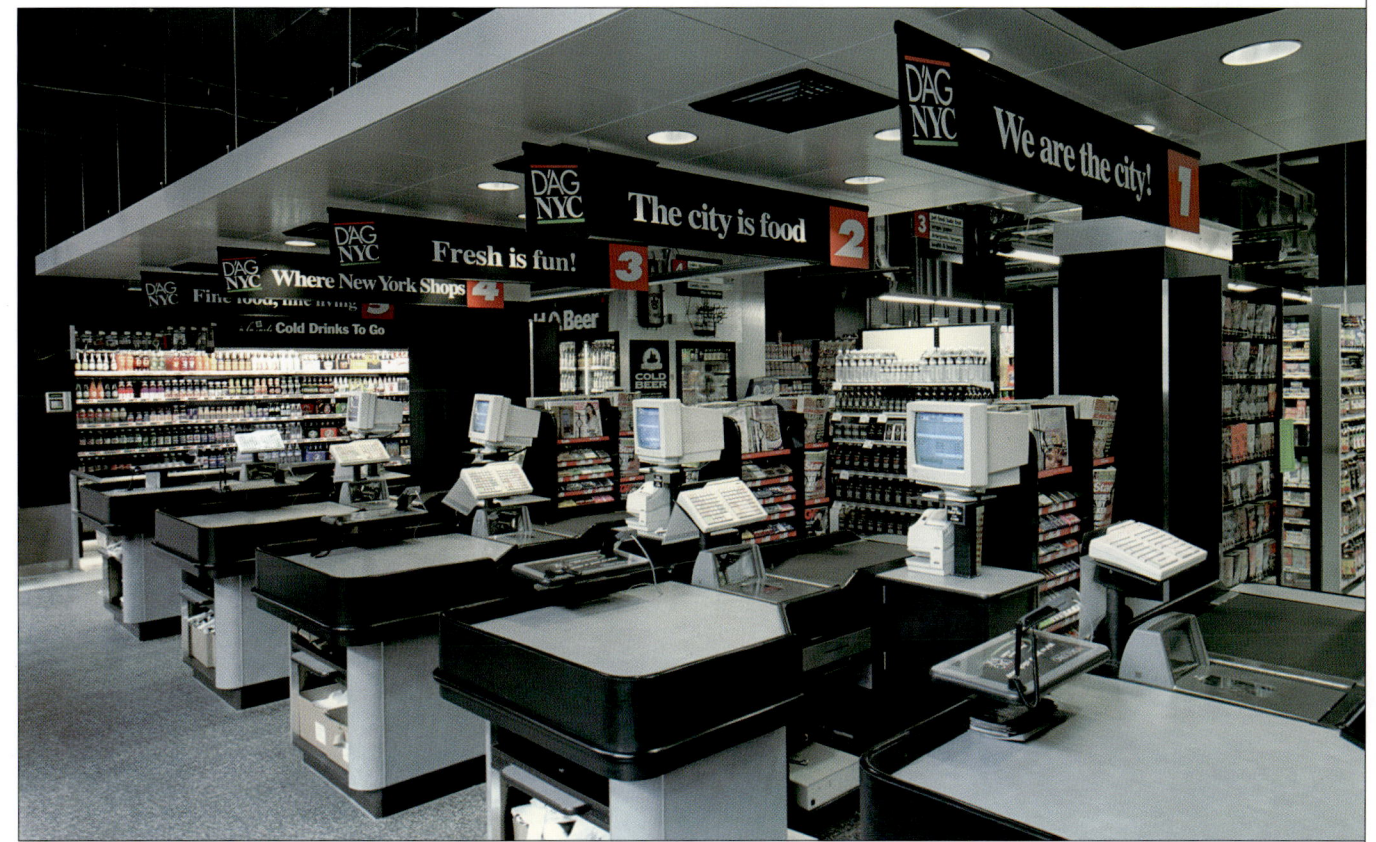

Above: Five check-out lanes, identified and illuminated, with scanning capabilities that speed up the process.

Top: The beer cooler is near check-out for easy access and convenience.

Watt IDG

Jumbo
Mendoza, Argentina

Jumbo is a hypermarket chain famous throughout the Argentine and this 142,000 sq. ft. giant market in Mendoza is the newest addition and serves as the mall's anchor store. Watt IDG designed a distinctive and coherent signage program that combines huge photographic images of food products with the departmental names. These heroic panels appear on the soffit over the color coordinated tiled walls of the service shops. In some areas heavy timber grids are hung down from the high, white open deck ceiling which is divided up by crisscrossing frameworks of trusses and beams. These dropped grids help to identify featured shops or areas in the store like in the brick-and-arched winery or the toiletries island in mid-floor.

A variety of colors are used to delineate and distinguish areas; primarily they are variations on earth colors: beige, tan, rust and terra-cotta. There are some zones accented with yellow (cheese), red (meat) and seafoam blue (fish). A deep green band appears on the fascia between the colored walls and the giant departmental signs above. The marmoleum covered floors range from dark taupe in produce to plum in winery, mauve and yellow in fashion and soft orange in seasonal. Light tan takes over most of the other areas. Metal halide lamps in market-style fixtures are used throughout to light up the vast space.

Above: Green canvas awnings highlight the produce area.
Below: A wood grid accentuates the toiletries island.

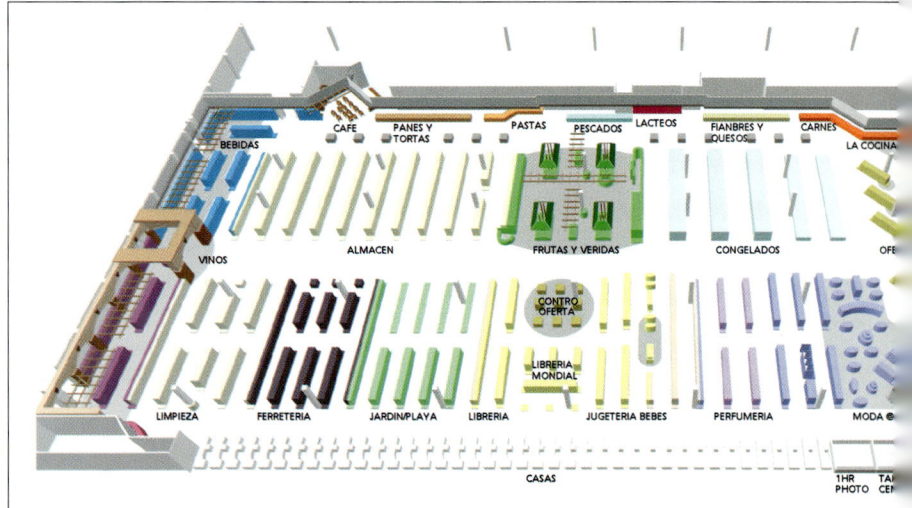

Above & center: The giant graphic signs dominate above the green fascia and mark off the service areas. Colored wall tiles—blue in fish and red in meat—also distinguish each shop.
Below: The winery has "brick" piers to support the terra-cotta aches. Faux windows add to the look as does the ceiling grid through which metal halide lamps are dropped.
Photography: Jumbo.
Illustration: Matt DeAbreu.

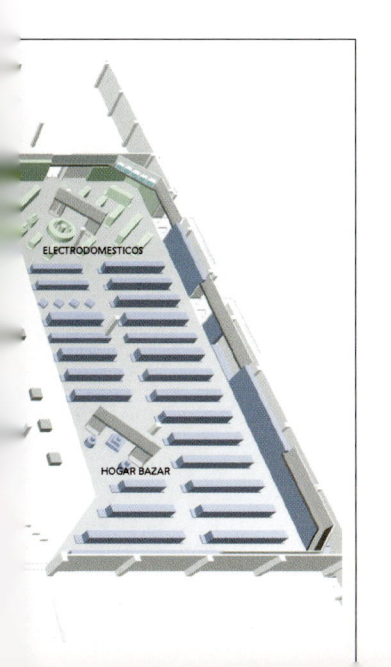

Watt IDG

Longo's
Mississauga, Ontario
Canada

Above: The white and red accented entrance into Longo's.
Below: A wide angle view of the spacious market with produce up front. Note the identifying signage and the multitude of hanging lamps.

In a new shopping plaza in Mississauga, this new Longo's joins 13 other stores in the family-owned chain of supermarkets. The white facade steps forward under a sweeping, arced aluminum roof with a tier of clerestory windows beneath it. This entrance is faced with 2 ft. x 4 ft. Arriscraft masonry blocks and accented with the Longo's signature in red. A slash of red accentuates the marquee over the doors. Set back is the red brick building that is about 24 ft. high. The bright red accent continues as a rain/sun cover along the side of the building. Its "clean, contemporary presence" ties in with the rest of the shopping plaza and the surrounding neighborhood.

Inside the 31,000 sq. ft. space seems spacious—and endless. The white open deck ceiling is filled with the HVAC systems and ductwork and supports the hundreds of metal halide lamps that drop down over all the merchandised areas. The well-designed and oversized signage is readily seen from almost anywhere in the market and "is used to inform and support the brand name and set the tone for the department." In the produce area individual items such as apples and potatoes get special rectangular signs enriched with strong, bright colored photographic collages.

The produce area is further enhanced by a wall mural composed of giant blow-ups of old farm scenes. They add a contrast to the contemporary setting while complementing the stained wood accents in the area such as the farm stand platforms and island units sitting on the porcelain tile floor.

Above: The potatoes photographic sign highlights the assortment of potatoes set out below it. Behind is the wall mural of greatly enlarged antique photos of farm scenes.
Photography:
Richard Johnson, Interior Images

Above: *The kitchen where prepared cooked foods are ready to-go. In the background, the prepared produce to-go at Fresh & Ready.*

Throughout this Longo's, the designers used a variety of textures and materials to create interest as well as to distinguish individual areas in the store. The kitchen is crowned with a giant hood with a mottled metallic finish that matches the facings on the cases up front. For this island, the prep wall is faced with cultured river stones and green shutters surround the ovens and rotisseries. Here, too, photographic images were used—above eye level—to identify the area for shoppers. From the kitchen comes ready-to-go meals and there is a great variety of prepared foods. Especially signed is Kama Sushi which is part of this island shop. Seating is provided nearby so that shoppers can snack or lunch on these cooked foods.

Another highlighted area is Fresh and Ready—prepared fresh produce. Green canvas canopies top the mottled brown laminate faced counters that carry the fresh salads and soups. Set along the yellow tiled wall under an heroic sized green awning are the pre-packaged selections. On a heavy timber grid hanging between the wall counters and the free-standing islands is a colorful display of fruits, vegetables and decorative, farm related props. In Longo's the designers have "created a fresh food experience that captivates the consumers and creates a unique and rewarding shopping opportunity."

This page: Green awnings and canopies, yellow tiled walls, mottled brown laminate cases and accents of Longo's signature red together create a strong presence for Fresh & Ready.

Watt IDG

ICA Kvantum
Enköping, Sweden

In Enköping, ICA Kvantum built a new 2500 sq. ft. market and Watt IDG's primary role was in developing "an integrated communications platform ... Since the opening, we have developed complete departmental concepts for all departments, attempting to balance the requirement to upgrade the experience of the environment with the price perception—in an extremely price-point competitive environment." Adding to the problem, the client was operating within fixed budgetary restraints and high local labor costs. These issues were addressed by Watt IDG by presenting self-serviced environments—resembling service departments—while "using communication elements to reduce the consumer's need for direct associate contact." Though the exterior is red with white trim, the interior is mainly neutral in color with gray and white vinyl composition tiles on the floor. To make the store environment come alive, the designers combined photographic imagery with departmental identification and all the colors "contribute to a more clearly articulated and inspirational environment." Here "the product takes center stage." In future developments ambient illustrations will appear on perimeter bulkheads—related to the adjacent departments—and "profile" departments will be augmented with specialized floor treatments and customized tile

Above: The red facade of IVA Kvantum highlighted by giant food photomurals.
Below: The open ceiling has exposed laminated wood beans and painted metal structural elements.
Photography: Hans Nilsson
Illustration: Matt De Arbeau

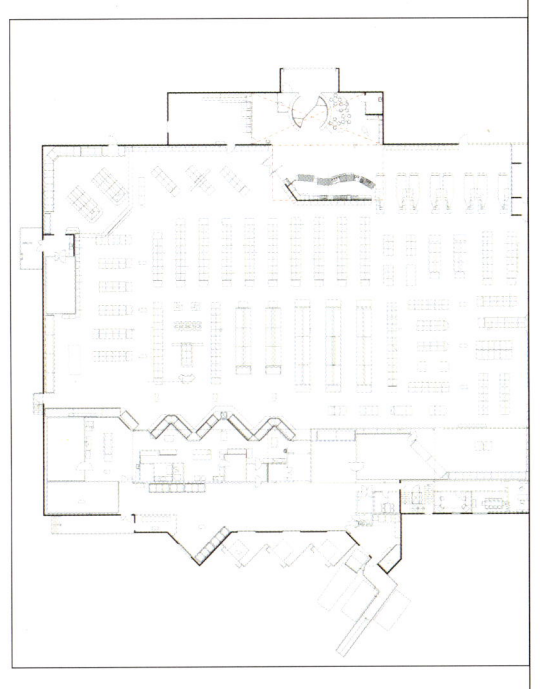

patterns. This is a work in progress. "The next iteration of the concept should go a long way to delivering an unprecedented food shopping experience in the local market."

This page: Examples of the hanging signage that was devised to ease the shopping experience while adding to the ambiance of the market.

Watt IDG

Soriana
San Pedro, Monterrey
Nuevo Leon, Mexico

This super-scaled, hypermarket that serves as a flagship and an anchor for an established shopping center is one of the 110-store Soriana hypermarket chain. Watt IDG was invited to create a whole new look for this 15 year old store which boasts of a spectacular 50 ft. high x 55 ft. wide circular, glazed entranceway. Watt, working with Soriana's executive management, developed "a new product-driven retail environment that positions the business effectively through merchandising and integrated communications." For this store with 90,000 sq. ft. devoted to sales, the designers devised a "customer-centric shopping experience that is convenient and recognizes the customer's purchase requirements." A logical traffic flow was created and departmental adjacencies reconsidered for maximum efficiency. Throughout, focal points and vistas were established to draw customers along the shorter and more inviting aisles which were also made wider. Overstock was removed from the top shelves so that more light could illuminate the product and create the feeling of greater space. Merchandise was zoned to allow customers a more flexible and convenient store experience and to encourage cross selling by grouping departments with like products.

Above: The bold sweep of the blue glass and blue and silver Alucoband-faced entrance into Soriana. **Left:** The turquoise and off-white checkerboard floor marks off the produce department. The luxalon grid overhead carries spots and fluorescent lay-in fixtures.
Photography: Gorge Taboada

Left: The bakery is distinguished by a wide, curving soffit with a red/orange band and a green stripe. An icon and the department name are overlaid. Natural wood fixtures sweep out in front of the brick ovens.
Below: A puddle of blue flooring complements the cool blue soffit treatment over the fish department.

167

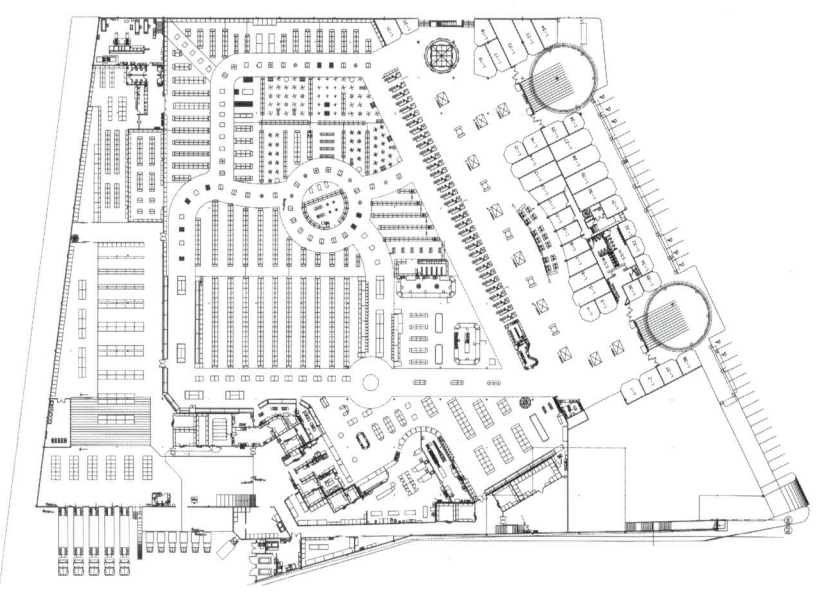

Above: The skylight walkway through the groceries area leading to Fresh Market.
Below: A luxalon grid, draped with clusters of grapes and leaves, hangs over the woody ambiance of the wine shop.

A 25 ft. wide by 150 ft. long skylight directs shoppers into the Fresh Market. Handsome, angled wood gondolas with blackboard signs on top show off the featured groceries along the way. In the Fresh Market area the designers used a three ft. wide band of an appropriate color to distinguish each shop. The color is related to the product: blue for fish, red/orange for baked goods, green for produce, red for meat, etc. The product name is used as a repeat pattern on the band which is further highlighted by an icon of the product and the name of the department. A continuous stripe of Soriana's corporate green color ties the whole area together. The interior is alive with color and light from the corn yellow walls to the vinyl tiles that include sun gold, turquoise, blue, cactus and lime green, almond, mango orange and burgundy red. 400-watt metal halide lamps are used for general lighting along with 2 ft. x 2 ft. recessed fluorescents and adjustable track lights including 70 watt par 30 metal halide lamps. The new, colorful and welcoming design not only addressed the requirements of Soriana's existing customer base but has proven to be a great draw for new shoppers.

From Floor To Ceiling…
Solutions For The Supermarket Environment.

Power It

Boston Retail's power products are designed to cut installation costs during store construction and remodeling. All components are delivered as a "kit" for quick and easy installation for your contractors. Less on-site wire terminations mean less time and labor on the job.

Protect It

Boston Retail's full line of damage protection products is designed to protect walls, fixtures and expensive refrigeration units from costly damage. The entire line is available in a broad array of colors, sizes and styles to protect and enhance your customer's shopping experience.

Display It

Boston Retail's merchandising display fixtures let you present product on your selling floor uniquely and safely. Because every installation is unique, Boston Retail's experienced engineering team works side-by-side with each customer to develop solutions by designing and manufacturing units that are exclusive to their environment.

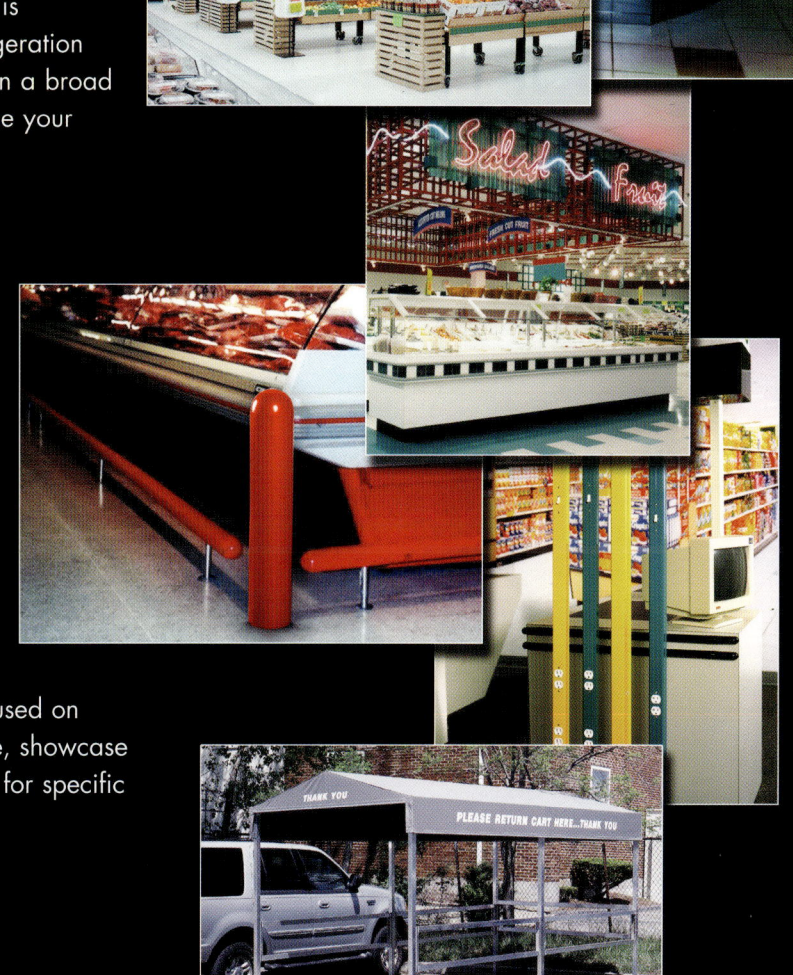

Depend On It

For more than 60 years Boston Retail Products has focused on providing innovative solutions that enhance your image, showcase your products, and protect your investment. Contact us for specific product information today.

Boston Retail Products

800-225-1633 • www.bostonretail.com • 400 Riverside Avenue • Medford, MA 02155 • Email: info@bostonretail.com

Index by Projects

Akbar's Café, New York, NY, **21**

Albertson's, Jackson Hole, WY, **26**

Alfredo's Marketplace Associated, Wyandanch, NY, **18**

Amelia's Market, Four Seasons, IN, **22**

Blue Sage Supermarket, El Paso, TX, **148**

Bonson's Pick n'Save, Eagle River, WI, **128**

Busch's Marketplace, Livonia, MI, **130**

Busch's, Farmington Hills, MI, **122**

City Market, Vail, CO, **34**

Copps Food Center, Neenah, WI, **36**

D'Agostino, 54th Street & 10th Ave., New York, NY, **154**

Danube Supermarket 3 Tahalia, Jeddah, Saudi Arabia, **48**

Danube Supermarket 4 Nahda, Jeddah, Saudi Arabia, **52**

Danube Supermarket 5 Arbaeen, Jeddah, Saudi Arabia, **42**

Delchamps Primier, Mandeville, LA, **112**

Evan's Supermarket, Detroit Lakes, MN, **14**

Flagship concept, Randalls # 64 Bellaire, TX, Randalls # 11 Houston, TX, **74**

Flexible concept, Randalls # 480 Austin, TX, **78**

Food Maxx, San Leandro, CA, **146**

Gelson's, Irvine, CA, **102**

Gelson's, Pasadena, CA, **90**

Gourmet Garage, Scarsdale, NY, **118**

Grande, Trujillo Alto, Puerto Rico, **110**

Guiliano's Fresh, Norfolk, VA, **116**

Harmon's Market, Vandalia, IL, **60**

ICA Kvantum, Enköping, Sweden, **164**

Jensen's Finest Foods, La Quinta, CA, **94**

Jumbo, Mendoza, Argentina, **158**

Longo's, Mississauga, ON, Canada, **160**

Market of Choice, Ashland, OR, **100**

Nelson's Supermarket, North Branch, MN, **12**

New Generatio, Exterior Options, **86**

New Generation, Prototype Design, **82**

Next Generation, Prototypical Shell Designs, **88**

Nob Hill Foods, Salinas, CA, **96**

Park View Market, Bradford, PA, **16**

Pick 'n Save River Edge, Wausau, WI, **62**

Pick 'n Save, Mukwanago, WI, **68**

Pick 'n Save, Zaneville, OH, **58**

Price Chopper, Plattsburgh, NY, **114**

PSK Foodtown, Brooklyn, NY, **120**

Quality Foods, Comox, BC, Canada, **106**

Racemart, Raceway Petroleum, Highland Park, NJ, **20**

Rouse Epicurian Market, Thibodaux, LA, **10**

Safeway Inc., USA and Canada, **92**

Save Mart Supermarket, Clovis, CA, **138**

Seattle Coffee, Penn Station, New York, NY, **19**

Sendik's Food Market, Brookfield, WI, **134**

Sentry Foods — Hilldale, Madison, WI, **126**

Sentry Foods, Walworth, WI, **132**

Soriana, San Pedro, Monterrey, Nuevo Leon, Mexico, **166**

Steele's Market, Fort Collins, CO, **70**

Sunmart, Moorhead, MN, **66**

Super One Foods, Duluth, MN, **150**

Supermercados Unicasa, C.A., ESP Margarita— EDO.NUEVA, Venezuela, **104**

Thrifty Foods, Tsawwassen, Delta, BC, Canada, **98**

Trigs Food & Drug, Eagle River, WI, **30**

Vista Mercado, El Paso, TX, **142**

Keep 100%,

GRADE A

profits from

evaporating

into thin air.

A product of Hill PHOENIX®
For more information call 770.285.3261 • www.hillphoenix.com

PARK AVENUE
PRESTIGE